FALKIRK AND DISTRICT

AN ILLUSTRATED ARCHITECTURAL GUIDE

As a born and bred Falkirk 'bairn', I was delighted to pen this foreword.

In studying the content, I was instantly transported to my childhood, recalling many of the buildings as they were formerly used and reflecting upon their evolution. Familiarity, though, can lead to taking one's surroundings for granted and to this I must plead guilty. However, in revisiting the area through this guide, I am re-awakened to the diversity of its architecture.

From modest miner's cottage to grand château, from canal to foundry, the guide records the area's history as manifest in the built form, often unearthing hidden treasures – hitherto underestimated in respect of their historical significance.

At a time when development within the area is rapidly expanding, one is encouraged to become reacquainted with its architectural heritage, which is no bad thing.

I feel sure that fellow 'bairn' and visitor alike will be enlightened by this well-researched guide and, hopefully, become more engaged with the area's built heritage, past and present.

Sam Sweeney
President, Stirling Society of Architects

D0003306

© Author: Richard Jaques
Series editor: Charles McKean
Series consultant: David Walker
Index: Oula Jones
Cover design: The Almond Consultancy

Cover illustrations
Front Callendar House (Falkirk Council).
Back Elphinstone Tower, Dunmore (Richard Jaques).
Inset Town Hall and Carnegie Library and Victorian Bandstand, Bo'ness (Argyll, the Isles, Loch Lomond, Stirling & Trossachs Tourist Board).

The Rutland Press
ISBN 1873190085
1st published 2001

Typesetting and picture scans by
The Almond Consultancy, Edinburgh
Printed by The Cromwell Press, Trowbridge, Wiltshire

British Library Cataloguing in Publication Data.
A catalogue record for this book is available from the British Library.

A crook of the Forth is worth an earldom in the North
Old Scottish saying

Situated at the heart of the central belt, Falkirk
and district stretches from the rich agricultural
carselands of Dunmore and Airth in the north to
the bleak but characterful moorlands surrounding
Slamannan and Avonbridge in the south; from
Denny and Dunipace, and the watershed of
Carron in the west to the scenic gorge of the Avon
in the east. At the centre lies Falkirk with its
independent satellites of Camelon, Larbert,
Stenhousemuir, Carron, Laurieston, Polmont and
Hallglen, while the wide waters of the Firth of
Forth wash the northern boundary from South
Alloa to Bo'ness giving this part of the district a
distinctive maritime flavour.

Detail, Polmont Old Parish Church.

As with neighbouring West Lothian, there are
no great mountain ranges, the ground rising
gently from the coastal strip, with its distinctive
raised beaches at Bo'ness and Grangemouth to
the moorlands in the south. Apart from Darroch
Hill to the west of Denny, the few isolated
eminences, such as those at Dunmore, Kinnaird,
Dunipace and Torwood (the latter the location of
one of the few Lowland brochs), speak of
volcanic activity in prehistoric eras, while
important fossil finds at Camelon confirm that at
one time the waters of the Forth estuary extended
far inland.

Following on from the example set by the royal
forest of Torwood, the west of the district is and
has always been more heavily wooded than the
east, where mining activity has inevitably greatly
impoverished the landscape. Today the district is
profiting by the national interest in reforestation,
including the great stretches of conifer plantings
in and around Limerigg to the south.

Three rivers, each very different in character,
drain this large inclined plain. To the north, the
Powburn wriggles its way between the mosses of
the carselands resulting in a landscape distinctly
Dutch in character; the swift-flowing Carron, over
25 miles long, and with almost as many twists and
turns as the Yangtze, rises in the Campsies to the
north of Glasgow before flowing into the Forth at
Grangemouth; and the Avon, deep in its gorge to
the south east and a challenge to the district's
bridge builders who have not been found wanting.
It is, of course, the abundant mineral wealth of the
area, particularly coal and iron ore, that has been
decisive in the district's more recent history.

Politically, as a result of its situation at the very
heart of Scotland's Lowlands, Falkirk and district
has literally been central to Scotland's history; a

Below *A crook of the Forth at Airth by
Timothy Pont c.1853–96.* Opposite *View
down School Brae, Bo'ness. (Jaques)*

*Top Scotland's Close, Bo'ness.
Above Brightons.*

*Detail, Parish Church of St Lawrence,
Slamannan.*

crossroads in pre-Christian times in the struggles between warring Celtic tribes, a sentinel between north and south at all times, and an area whose strategic importance to the Romans merited an extensive defensive vallum. It was also excellent guerrilla territory for William Wallace and Robert the Bruce in their early struggles with perfidious Albion, a spacious arena for Scots and English to fight it out in the days of the Rough Wooings, and finally a breathing space for the Young Pretender on the eve of his defeat at Culloden.

In quieter times, its central position saw Falkirk make its name as the location of the Tryst, the greatest of all the many cattle markets in Scotland. To agricultural importance was added industrial pre-eminence when Carron Iron Company's furnaces roared into life, heralding the great days of Scotland's status as an industrial nation, its maritime links being forged and maintained first through Bo'ness and then Grangemouth, while an excellent network of road, canal and rail distributed goods nationwide and opened up the nation culturally as it did so. Because of its history and geography, Falkirk is very much a hands-on working territory, one whose modern physiognomy has been cast largely by self-made men, by the inventor, engineer, iron founder, canal cutter, bridge builder and coal hewer. One is more likely to hear the names of John Smeaton, John Logie Baird and James Watt on people's lips rather than more conventional heroes. The gentlemen writers and scholars largely avoided the district, although Thomas Pennant came in 1769 and Robert Burns in 1787.

The great foundries and associated industries that grew up around Carron should not blind one to the great achievements of other parts of the district; of Denny and Dunipace for instance, utilising the soft waters of Carron in paper making, or of Bonnybridge in brick making and of all those unsung towns and villages from Polmont to Slamannan and Avonbridge that provided the coal essential to this industrial take-off. If their architectural heritage is relatively meagre, their importance is not. Without their contribution, the district would not be enjoying the standard of life it enjoys today.

Overlaid by this 250 years of industrial endeavour is a land with an abundance of romantic castles, including those at Almond, Airth, Torwood and Castlecary and of great houses, such as Kinneil, Callendar and Dunmore (with its famous Pineapple folly) and their equally great families, the Dukes of Hamilton, the Livingstones and the

Elphinstones of Airth. At Kinnaird the maverick figure of James Bruce, 'The Abyssinian Traveller', bestrides the scene like a colossus.

Alongside castle and mansion is the architecture of the vernacular, such as at the former royal port of Airth and the planned villages of Dunmore and of Muirhouses near Carriden. Architectural interest too is to be found in the contrasting towns of Grangemouth and Bo'ness, in the socially innovative village of Westquarter, in the pioneering and internationally acclaimed hospitals of Falkirk, Larbert and Bellsdyke, and in the glittering high-tech buildings of Callendar Business Park.

Local architectural heroes such as William Black, J G Callender and Thomas Copland in Falkirk, and Matthew Steele and James Thomson in Bo'ness, rub shoulders with such nationally important figures as William Wilkins, Sir John James Burnet, Sir Robert Rowand Anderson, Frederick Thomas Pilkington and J M MacLaren, while international luminary Sir Norman Foster, somewhat unexpectedly, adds the spice of high-tech wizardry at Bellsdyke.

Evidence of the district's regeneration over recent years is abundant, spanning the spectrum of cultural, environmental and leisure initiatives. The five new PFI schools, now up and running, the museums at Falkirk, Kinneil and Grangemouth, the Heritage Site at Bo'ness, new road systems and business parks at Falkirk and Bellsdyke all attest to a new sense of vigour and direction. If any one symbol is required of an area that once again, after many vicissitudes is holding its head up high, it must be the Falkirk Wheel at Camelon, a 21st-century triumph of engineering and Falkirk's answer to the London Eye – an achievement to equal those of the great 19th- and 20th-century engineers. Falkirk and district's new era is well underway – its architectural re-awakening and renaissance only a matter of time.

Organisation of this guide

The guide begins at Falkirk itself, then passes through Larbert, Stenhousemuir, Carron and Airth, arriving in the carselands of the north at Dunmore. From there Torwood provides the link to Denny and the west, the route returning by Bonnybridge and the east. From Polmont, the old drove road leads south to Muiravonside, Brightons and Maddiston, climbing up across the moors to Limeriggs, Avonbridge and Slamannan. The guide ends at the coast, taking in Grangemouth, Kinneil and Bo'ness before finishing at Carriden near the A904.

Top *Interior of entrance portico, The Pineapple, Dunmore.* Above *Former tolbooth, 13 South Street, Bo'ness.*

Plaque on new Millennium Link bridges.

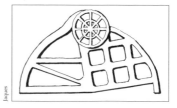

Section, Falkirk Wheel.

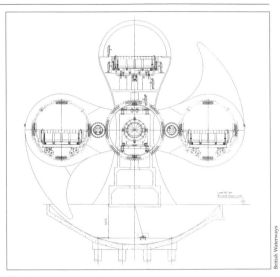

British Waterways

Text arrangement
Entries for principal buildings follow the sequence of name (or number), address, date and architect (if known). Lesser buildings are contained within paragraphs. Both demolished buildings and unrealised projects are included if appropriate. In general, the dates given are those of the design (if known) or of the beginning of construction. Entries in the small column highlight interesting biographical, historical and social aspects of the story of Falkirk and district.

Map References
Maps are included for the towns, with a larger map covering the whole area. Numbers on the maps do not refer to pages but to the small numbers adjacent to the text itself. Numbers in the index refer to pages.

Access to Properties
The majority of buildings in this guide are visible from public roads or footpaths. However, only a few of them are normally open for public visiting, and readers are requested to respect the occupiers' privacy.

Sponsors
The generous support is gratefully acknowledged of Falkirk Environment Trust, former Ossory Estates, Argyll, the Isles, Loch Lomond, Stirling & Trossachs Tourist Board, former Central Regional Council, former Falkirk District Council, Pollock Hammond Partnership, Gordon Fraser Charitable Trust and The Landmark Trust.

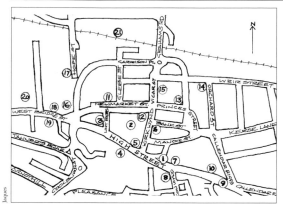

Jaques

The earliest recorded history of Roman Falkirk begins in 82 AD when the Roman General Agricola launched his invasion of Caledonia. He built a line of forts from the Forth to the Clyde in order to keep the wild natives at bay and to protect his legions. This was later replaced by the **Antonine Wall**, a ditch and rampart fortification. Within today's Falkirk, the line of the wall passes by way of Callendar Park, Arnothill and Camelon. Further west it is at Watling Lodge and Rough Castle, that the best surviving sections are to be found.

FALKIRK

Despite being the site of a fort astride a defensive ridge in Roman days, Falkirk rarely enters the history books, apart from the first Battle of Falkirk in 1298, until 1600, when the town of the 'Faw' or 'Spotted Kirk', became a burgh of barony.

Like Linlithgow, medieval in layout, at one time boasting a town wall it remained a one-street town, although an important one on the turnpike road connecting Edinburgh, Glasgow and Stirling, until Victorian times when a secondary loop was added by way of Newmarket Street. Callendar House, home of the Livingston family, principal landowners, remained discreetly outside town, a mile to the east.

Falkirk from near Falkirk High Station, c.1860.

Glasgow Art Gallery and Museum

Above *Map of Falkirk by Timothy Pont, c.1583–96.* Right *Forth & Clyde Canal at Bainsford, with Carron Iron Company boat, c.1890.*

The Forth & Clyde Canal which operated between 1790 and 1962 was a major commercial artery between Grangemouth on the Forth and Bowling in Glasgow. In its eastern section it followed very much the line of the Antonine Wall. Its success prompted Edinburgh businessmen to establish the Edinburgh & Glasgow Union Canal Company in 1822, which took goods and building materials from Central Scotland to Edinburgh.

At Lock 16, Port Downie, the two canals joined in a system of 11 locks climbing 110ft, the only locks on the Union Canal. The thriving passenger service between Edinburgh and Glasgow at one time took under 13 hours, and cost one halfpenny. Further plans would have continued the canal in Edinburgh from Lothian Road via a series of locks to Leith. Commercial traffic ceased in 1963.

Today, leisure interests have prompted a huge revival of practical interest in the canals with their particular flora and fauna, their now tranquil towpaths, and reflecting waters.

In the wake of the **Carron Iron Company** in 1759, many other iron foundries sprang up throughout the district. One of which, the Falkirk Iron Company, was begun by ex-employees of Carron Iron Company in 1810, a fact which gives the lie to the idea that a workers' takeover is an exclusively modern phenomenon. Abbott's Foundry followed with further new foundries at the rate of one every five years, until at one time there were in excess of 20, the majority sited by the canal at Bainsford and Grahamston, with others at Camelon and Larbert, adjacent to the railway. The famous **Grahamston Foundry**, with its impressive gates (see p.27 and colour p.84) was always to the fore in the production of drainage goods.

The Forth & Clyde Canal, linking Glasgow and Grangemouth, came in the 1790s, followed by the Union Canal, linking Falkirk and Edinburgh, in the 1820s, the two eventually linked by 11 locks at Camelon west of the town. More than any other developments, the canals, together with the ever-burgeoning success of the Carron Iron Company and its followers, transformed the market town of the carse to a major centre of industry. The coming of the railways in mid-19th century changed everything again with the result that the future of Falkirk and its satellite towns and villages was assured.

In the mid-18th and early 19th centuries, development and expansion began first to the north, at Grahamston and Bainsford as Carron's iron furnaces roared into life in 1759. Before this, employment for townspeople had been in various trades, including tanning, weaving and brewing as well as in agriculture. Prior to industrialisation the great agricultural fair, The Tryst, after its move from Crieff, was held at Redding Muir and Rough Castle before moving finally to Stenhousemuir.

Today, Falkirk has expanded to provide houses for workers in its industries and services as well as dormitory accommodation for Glasgow and Edinburgh. Despite this, the original villages, including Camelon, Grahamston, Bainsford, Laurieston and Polmont still retain individual status and character. Falkirk, although lacking the more obvious topographical interests of Stirling or Linlithgow, possesses a noble church, an elegant and eyecatching steeple, a highly successful pedestrianised area, many beautiful and well-kept parks and perhaps the most impressive 'château' in Scotland.

The fact that Falkirk is seldom visited by Edinburgh and Glasgow folk, and then usually by default, when the train breaks down, says more about the insular nature of the inhabitants of Scotland's two major cities than about the merits of Falkirk. This neglect is undeserved bearing in mind that it was here that Scotland's industrial history began and here that its wealth was made.

Nor will anyone who visits Falkirk today fail to be impressed by the superb quality of landscaping throughout the town. Whether this is a consequence of the lessons learned in the magnificent gardens of the Callendar estate or of the existence of an enlightened landscape department, evidence is everywhere; the usual fussy efforts of the typical municipal department are here replaced by bold and imaginative swathes of colour and greenery, an endeavour acknowledged over the years by many awards, including Britain in Bloom Award, 1990 (see colour p.81).

Falkirk's Town Wall
It is statute and ordanit that ilk quarter of the toune of Falkirk come forth dey aboute for buildeing of ane dyk about the said burgh for keipeing forthe of streingeris sua that nane mey enter bot at the ports thairof viz. the eist and west portis kirkwynd pantaskenes wynde and kow wynde.
MS Court Book of Falkirk, 1647

Left *Steeple*. Below *David Hamilton's original drawing*.

1 Steeple, 1813–14, David Hamilton
The most outstanding landmark in Falkirk, 140ft high and visible for miles, the third such building erected on the site and a distinguished classical centrepiece to Falkirk's market place. Four

John Russell of Falkirk was one of the best watchmakers of his generation. He was appointed Watchmaker in Scotland to the Prince of Wales (later King George IV) in the 1790s. The burgh of Falkirk decided in 1813 to rebuild the Town House and Russell was asked to make the clock for the Steeple. Built in 1815, it remained in use until 1927 when the Steeple was partly destroyed by lightning. Comprising four 6ft diameter faces, originally solid but later glazed to be visible at night. Reconstruction of two faces and mechanism can be seen at the Royal Museum of Scotland, Edinburgh.

Dating from the 17th century, the elected representatives of the merchants and traders were known as stentmasters. They met from time to time 'to cast the stent', i.e. to fix the rates to be levied, mainly in the early years for water. Payment depended on a person's income rather than his property.

Another power group was **the feuars**, those who held property in the town. The history of the town's local politics is the struggle between these two power blocs to gain control of the town's affairs. If the stentmasters could point to the Steeple by way of achievement, the feuars responded by pointing to the Corn Exchange. Following the reform acts of the 1830s, the stentmasters reluctantly handed over their powers to the new town council, as did the feuars, some 40 years later.

Cross Well.

beautifully proportioned stages of finely detailed ashlar include ground floor (originally intended to be a shop), jailor's room on first floor, fully glazed second stage, pilastered four-clock third stage (clocks originally by John Russell) and octagonal belfry with Ionic columns and louvres, with spire topped by golden cockerel weathervane. Built by Henry Taylor, a local builder, for the Stentmasters of Falkirk (for £1,460) to contain prison cells to house *strolling vagrants and people who commit petty crimes*. In 1927, top 30ft was struck by lightning and collapsed killing a horse, and was rebuilt.

Mercat Cross
Site of original mercat cross, marked by a cross within a circle in the causeway setts. Here were held weekly markets, proclamations and hangings, the last of the latter in 1826.

Cross Well, 1817
Rebuild of the well donated by the Livingstons of Callendar *to the wives and bairns of Falkirk* in 1681. Circular, in stone, with plaque and domed top surmounted by the original lion displaying a shield containing the Livingston arms. In storage for 10 years after a lorry ran into it – to be erected adjacent to Howgate Centre, 2002.

Tolbooth Street, very narrow and characterful, sneaks behind the Steeple, a plaque recording it as being *the shortest street in Great Britain at a length of 5ft*. **Fleshmarket Close**, almost as narrow, formerly one of the principal shambles in days of yore and gore. **Wooer Street**, east of the Steeple, derives its name from the old Scots word for a weaver, its narrow and setted confines providing interesting and surprising views of the Steeple and its surroundings: with Tolbooth Street and Fleshmarket Close, a more obviously picturesque part of town. Here, traditionally, weavers, butchers and assorted trades had their businesses. Modern development on east side has happily respected the small-scale character of the area.

Mini-precinct, High Street
Gap site, with view of Old Parish Church, giving welcome break in busy street. Between gables to tenement ends, seats and planters, arched **gateway**, 1659, with 19th-century cast-iron gothic gates. Civic Trust Award, 1960.

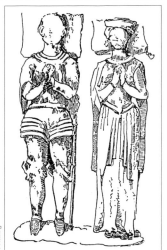

2 Falkirk Old and St Modan's Parish Church,
High Street, from 15th century

Darkly ensconced on tree-enshrouded central site, Falkirk's 'Spotted Kirk' remains surprisingly unified despite hotch-potch of additions, including 1738 William Adam remodelling of the crossing of the old church with stone octagonal belfry and elegant swept spire, now serving as vestibule to James Gillespie Graham's large new church of 1810 to the north. In sombre grey rubble, with crenellated parapet, crowstepped gables and Y-tracery to its windows, it contains handsome horseshoe balcony supported on wooden columns and approached by graceful curving stair. Within, two **medieval effigies**, including one of Sir Alexander Livingston, died 1467. Somewhat academic south transept and *porte-cochère* added, 1892, by Sir Robert Rowand Anderson.

Outside, **memorials** to those killed at the First Battle of Falkirk in 1298, Sir John de Graeme and Sir John Stewart of Bonkhill; Graeme tomb, much rebuilt, has delicate gothic ironwork and decorative crown top. **Bute memorial**, 1877, Mossmans, large Celtic cross with lacy lattice design in memory of the men of Bute.

High Street
Falkirk's High Street, like Linlithgow's, has long been the main artery of the town and the typical fish-bone plan, with narrow wynds leading off north and south, can still be discerned. Few old wynds remain except Cow, Bell and Baxter's Wynd, and the dignified King's Court; Sword's Wynd and Robert's

Left *Old Parish Church.* Top *Medieval effigies, probably of Lord William Livingstone and wife, c.1590.* Above *Sir John de Graeme tomb.*

Sir John de Graeme, William Wallace's right hand man at the First Battle of Falkirk in 1298, had fought with him at the Battle of Stirling Bridge the previous year. Blind Harry's account, 1508, tells how de Graeme fought and died and has it that Wallace sought out the body and carried it to the churchyard at Falkirk for burial.

My faithful friend when I was hardest stead
My hope, my health, thou wast in most honour
My faith, my health, my strenthiest in stoure
In thee was wit, freedom and hardness
In thee was truth, manhood and nobleness
In thee was rule, in thee was governing
In thee virtue without varying
In thee was loyalty, in thee was largesse
In thee gentility, in thee was steadfastness
They carried him with worship and dolour
Into Fawkirk graith'd him in sepulture.

11

FALKIRK – High Street

High Street c.1895.

Wynd, for instance, have been subsumed into the Howgate Centre.

As the wynds, so too the architecture. Few old buildings remain, most being 19th or 20th century. Pedestrianised, 1988–9, with red paviors, planters, trees and decorative lighting standards, the street is now a model of its kind having a focus at the Steeple, where its line is subtly inflected, closing the vistas and making for a good sense of enclosure. Further west, an open space gives onto the Old Parish Church, while east of the Steeple the homely Cow Wynd wends its way south. In general, the street follows a natural ridge with steepish falls to East Bridge Street and West Bridge Street.

Below *Marshall Wilson*. Bottom *Doorway, Royal Hotel.*

Marshall Wilson, No 2, 1879, Peddie and Kinnear
Picturesque Scots Baronial former Royal Bank Buildings in brown rubble on corner site; three storeys, two-storey oriel to gushet, dormers to High Street and steeply pitched and slated roofs behind crowstepped gables.

Royal Hotel, *c.*1760
Two storey, painted and quoined with Ionic doorpiece in channelled ground-floor stonework.

3 **Lint Riggs**, 1903 onwards, David Ronald, Burgh Engineer
The well-articulated streetscape of Lint Riggs is dramatically signalled at High Street by two projecting and ogee-domed turrets, one in copper with mini-temple cupola, the other in lead with flagpole; both have decorative stone panels to their chamfered waistlines below the domes. Formerly very narrow, not more than a few feet across, with iron gate onto High Street, the name deriving from the old Falkirk linen industry.

A municipally promoted improvement, like Whitehall Street in Dundee which probably was its inspiration (see *Dundee* in this series); three storeys of well-detailed and well-proportioned angled bays with parapets and fluted wallhead chimneys, all in creamy stonework, make for excellent streetscape. Elegant façades and more corner turrets extend into Newmarket Street. **The Goose on Newmarket** bar has angled corner bay and impressive frontage between Corinthian pilasters.

Temperance Café (former Crown Hotel)
Heavily consoled and pedimented porch with square black marble columns gives access to what was the alleged location for the first public demonstration of television in Scotland, November 1927.

Masonic Hall, 1906, Copland & Blakey, A & W Black
A departure from the rest of the block in the treatment of the frontage, segmented pediment, pilasters and balustraded doorpiece inscribed *Masonic Temple No 588, Lodge Callendar*. Inside, at first floor and approached by way of stair with green and white *wally* (china) tiles of the period, sombre but intriguing green and orange interior based, as is standard, on the proportions of Solomon's temple. Much traditional symbolism, including all-seeing eye, trade insignia and five magnificent coloured glass windows with wing motif. Sinuous Art Nouveau brass wall and hanging lamps suggest Copland was responsible for the furnishing (see The Hatherley, p.38).

Marks & Spencers, 1937, Robert Lutyens
Designed by Edwin Lutyens' son in neo-Georgian, with well-proportioned window groupings set in chequerboard cladding and prim but decisive cornicing.

Top *Lint Riggs*. Middle *The Goose on Newmarket*. Left *Masonic Hall*. Above *Doorway, Temperance Café*.

John Logie Baird, 1886–1946
Although the family came from Camelon, Baird was born in Helensburgh. After studying at Glasgow's Royal Technical College he pursued a very strange early career which included running a jam factory in Trinidad. He then returned to the south of England, living variously in London and Hastings.

He maintained a friendship with one John Hart of Falkirk, a businessman who had a radio supplies shop, first in the Pleasance and then in the High Street. It is alleged that the first demonstration of television took place in Falkirk's Temperance Café in Lint Riggs, although the documentation for this is meagre indeed.

Former Mathieson's Bakery, Shop and **Restaurant**, No 73, 1886
Unexpected treat from an old family business; four gently arched windows with leaded lights under pediment and date stone. Splendid shell apex crowned with a shield, bearing unicorn-rampant.

No 72, former Crawfords, boasts a whimsical pile of pediments, colour-washed frontage and curved glass shopfront.

4 **Howgate Centre**, 1990, Cockburn Associates Signalled by glazed canopy to High Street, multistorey shopping complex with parking below, shops above. In brick with mandatory glazed atria and glass lifts. Incorporated in main stair well, large and brilliantly coloured, **stained-glass windows**, formerly in South Bantaskine House, depicting Prince Charles Edward Stuart and his generals (see colour p.81).

5 **Kirk Wynd**
As with Lint Riggs, projecting towers signal the junction at Kirk Wynd, pepper-pot roof of one corner challenging sola topi of the other. Formerly Kirk Entry and one of five gates into

Top *73 High Street.* Above *Sword's Wynd c.1910.*

Sword's Wynd was where Bailie Sword, procurator fiscal for the burgh of regality in the 17th century, had his residence. Subsequently several inns and halls were built along this wynd and the **Baptist's Church of Christ** and the **Evangelical Union** had meeting rooms here. Steps led down to Howgate.

Right *High Street, Kirk Wynd and Royal Bank of Scotland.* Below *72 High Street.*

Falkirk. Originally no wider than could accommodate a cart, until the improvement schemes of 1904–10. Today a vital artery feeding into Grahamston and the north.

Royal Bank of Scotland, 1-9 Kirk Wynd, 1901, A Gauld
In fine red sandstone, robust, well-proportioned four-storey composition of pedimented and curved bays with crowned corner turret.

2 Kirk Wynd, *c.*1904, Thomas Copland
Three storey, red rubble, Scots Baronial former Railway Hotel, with crowstepped gable, corner turret and balcony.

Manor Street was, until 1896, Back Row, a secondary route running parallel to High Street along the foot of its gardens.

Manse Place, welcome breathing space giving steep access through pillared gateposts to parish churchyard, the manse long gone. Note turreted corner block, sculptural wall plaque, shell alcove above with 1895 **date stone**.

Bank Street
6 **Former Co-op Building**, 1931, J G Callender
Giant Egyptian orders, jazzy Art Deco ornamentation, burnished copper glazing spandrels and splayed corner bay with lozenge motif: 1930s' confidence at its commercial best. The Co-op boasted Falkirk's first lift for shoppers.

Former Salvation Army Citadel, 1910, (?)John Hamilton
Playful and confident exercise in brown rubble. Boldly stepped gable crowns wide-arched first-floor windows to hall. Steps lead to doorway with handsomely lettered name. Note inset subscription stones.

Britannic Assurance, 1985, Alan Jollie Associates
Well-mannered exercise in stone, slated roof and tinted glass with conservatory-style feature entrance.

Vision Express (formerly Saxone), 1965
Crisply detailed box over glazed shopfront.

Robert's Wynd, formerly Bantaskine Wynd, passed under one of the old ports leading out of Falkirk into the Pleasance, the most renowned building in which was **Rankine's Folly** built,

From top *Armorial panel, Royal Bank of Scotland; Former Co-op Building; Former Salvation Army Citadel; Vision Express.*

15

Top *Wilson's Buildings*. Above *123-127 High Street*.

The word **Baxter** derives from the old Scots word for baker. Bakers, candlemakers and butchers all plied their trades in Baxter's Wynd, though a decree of the Stentmasters in 1831 expressly forbade the slaughtering of animals on the premises.

On the east side of Baxter's Wynd, fronting High Street, stood formerly **The Great Lodging**, the town house of the Livingston family of Westquarter. It was here supposedly that Prince Charles Edward Stewart spent the night after the Second Battle of Falkirk in January 1746. The house was in existence until 1899.

Halifax Building Society (former Commercial Bank, *right*)
Love, in his *Antiquarian Notes and Queries* gives the architect as David Rhind. This seems unlikely as David Rhind was barely in practice at that date. James Gillespie Graham was then architect for the Commercial Bank's main provincial offices in Aberdeen and Stirling, for example.

1802, as assembly rooms. Repaired in 1852, it became the chief meeting place for many organisations and all manner of activities from church services to cock fighting (demolished).

Wilson's Buildings, 105-111 High Street, 1848 For John Wilson, coalmaster of South Bantaskine, four-storey ashlar giving the height and drama needed at this point in the streetscape with its hierarchical window treatment surmounted by name and date stone at roof level. Note rosette friezes at second-floor windows.

Wilson's Close, entered between modern shopfronts, has original arched entry at south end. **ScottishPower**, 1990s, cheerful, if ill-proportioned block with two storeys of cream wash and brown window surrounds.

113-117 High Street, early 19th century, three storeys, fine architraved windows with cornices, gives access to **Baxter's Wynd**. **W H Smith** (formerly Falkirk Herald building), Nos 123-127, 1909, three storeys of rusticated ashlar, canted bay windows flanking central bay with arched doorpiece and scrolled pediment. **Nos 129-131**, early 19th century, remodelled three storeys, five bays, quoined and painted stucco over modern shopfronts, first-floor windows attractively scrolled to cornice below. Pend leads to King's Court.

7 **Halifax Building Society**, 138 High Street, 1832, (?)James Gillespie Graham
Imposing visual stop to Cow Wynd, three-storey classical former Commercial Bank, comprising giant Ionic columns and pilastered flanking bays. Commendable restoration of ground floor; local design award, 1994.

King's Court is the best of the wynds, dark and Dickensian; a quiet haven after the bustle of High Street. Curves gracefully under its archway to reveal setted courtyard with 19th-century lamps and cast-iron **lion fountain**. Attractive modern additions include street names carved into paving slabs and wrought-iron window screens (see colour p.82).

Lloyds TSB Scotland, 1896, William Black
In Renaissance style, its rhythmic and arched windows and pedimented corner doorpiece, all in rusticated ashlar, give a certain distinction. Extended, 1926, J G Callender. Economy wing without cornicing and balustrading fronts onto Cow Wynd.

8 **Cow Wynd**
Joins High Street east of the Steeple, and was the only road to the south until early 20th century, its name coming from the route taken by drovers and their herds on the way up to the common muirs beyond Callendar Woods. Until 1770s, an essential route for such purposes in the years that the great Trysts were held in Falkirk (see Stenhousemuir p.56).

Top *King's Court.* Middle *Lion fountain.* Left *Tattie Kirk.* Above *Lloyds TSB Scotland.*

The Tattie Kirk, 1806
Visible from many vantage points and tucked behind Cow Wynd, octagonal plan (*no corner for the De'il to hide in*) in rubble with ashlar quoins and window margins, its shallow slated roof topped with replica urn finial by students of Falkirk Technical College. Formerly, gallery within, approached by external stone stair. A church of the Antiburgher Secession, last used as a church in 1879; now sawyer's store. To the south, its marooned **manse**. Similar churches at Kelso and Dundee (see *Borders & Berwick* and *Dundee* in this series).

5 & 7 Booth Place.

5 & 7 Booth Place, *c.*1830–40
Two well-detailed ashlar-fronted late Georgian cottages, with storey-height windows, add a touch of class to the street (named after a garden nursery owner), which provides the best views of the Tattie Kirk.

Russel & Aitken, 9 Cow Wynd, early 19th century
Tall, single storey, piended slate roof, interesting interior with rib vaulting on cast-iron columns. Extension, 1985, William A Cadell Architects, two-storey frontage with arched windows in sparkling exposed aggregate blocks.

Below *Russel & Aitken.* Bottom *Struthers Memorial Church.*

Barnton Lane and **Bean Row**, characterful back streets, with original setted surfaces in Barnton Lane, provide interesting views over King's Court to High Street including some fine semicircular stairtowers.

Struthers Memorial Church, Mission Lane, 1898
Italianate tower fronts four-bay hall of former Town Mission. Lack-lustre extension, 2001.

9 **High Street – east end**
On the south side, the street deteriorates architecturally. After the pend to **Dundee Court**, brash four-storey 1950s' block with 'potted meat' mosaic spandrel panels. Two good groups of four **terraced cottages**, later 19th century, two storey, colour washed and slated, end this section of High Street on the right homely and vernacular note.
  On first-floor frontage of A & J Mauchline Newsagents (former Cross Keys Inn), commemorative **plaque** with portrait head records that Robert Burns spent the night there during his visit to Falkirk on 25 August 1787.

Left *Callendar Square*. Above *Plaque, A & J Mauchline Newsagents.*

10 Callendar Square, 1995, Hasler Farthing, Newcastle, with Clark Tibble, USA
Large shopping complex, replacing Callendar Centre, 1961, Ardin & Brookes, with glazed atrium behind anaemic classical exterior in smooth cream render. Pediments to High Street and Callendar Riggs, domed corner tower. Two-storey glazed bridge links east façade to multistorey car park and J G Callender's bus station and shops, and acts as backdrop to the amenity of the new pedestrianised square with planters, seats and bandstand.

Bus Station and **Shops**, Callendar Riggs, 1935, J G Callender
Backing onto the bus station, range of two-storey shops includes three by this fine exponent of the Art Deco style. Much excellent patterning of the period including zigzags, chevrons and lozenges. Corner blocks intelligently handled, that to north including radiused black marble frontage, balcony recession and deeply curved cornice.

Come through the rich carse of Falkirk to Falkirk to pass the night was the entry made by Robert Burns on 25 August 1787 as he set out on his tour of the Highlands with his friend Willie Nicol. Staying the night at the Cross Keys Inn, they left early in the morning and after visiting the graveyard at the parish church, they went by way of Camelon, *ancient metropolis of the Picts* and the *Great Canal*, to Carron Iron Company. The plaque that records their stay was presented by William Thomson Mitchell of Grahamston Foundry and unveiled by Thomas Dawson Brodie of Carron Iron Company on 25 January 1889.

Nearby in the 1890s were the piggeries where the townspeople reared their pigs in *runs*. A rewarding and popular pastime in those days with pork at 6d a pound, pig-owners would scavenge the town for *brock*, the Scots for pig swill. Thus Falkirk's *Soo-logical Gardens* was the wag's name for this area.

Callendar Riggs.

J G Callender, d.1939, has some claim to be considered the Matthew Steele (see pp. 131-154) of Falkirk. As well as designing some fine shop frontages at Callendar Riggs he was responsible for the Co-op (p.15), the excellent curved block at Cockburn Street (p.25), and the offices of the Falkirk Iron Works in Graham's Road. In these and other works he combined a real understanding of the functional basis of 1930s' planning with a sure grasp of architecture's decorative possibilities.

Aitken's Brewery (*above*), Newmarket Street, 1900, Peter Lyle Henderson (demolished 1970)
Built on a site where brewing had taken place for some 150 years, James Aitken's Brewery, helped to slake the thirsts of Falkirk's ironworkers. Opened in 1900, its huge four and five-storey brick bulk all in a curious Franco-Scots château style, dwarfed the parish church and dominated the town.

Above *Wellington Statue*. Right *Registrar's Office and South African War Memorial.*

Falkirk's coat of arms has undergone many changes since the Reform Act of 1832, before which the town officials acted under the authority of the 'lairds of Callendar House'. From the earliest design depicting a lone Highlander, the design developed to that shown on the Burgh Buildings, the figures of two schoolchildren supporting a shield with the familiar bilingual scrolls *Tangite unum, tangite omnes* (Touch One, Touch All) and *Better meddle with the de'il than the bairns of Falkirk*. How the latter proverb came about is unknown. The more simplified designs of the 1970s depicts a shield and coronet, the shield quartered by the arms of Falkirk, Grangemouth, Bo'ness and Denny and Dunipace, the scrolls reduced to a simple *Ane for 'a.*

Newmarket Street
Previously a rough track across the parish church glebe, its name originates from the grain market established there in 1830. Today, vies with High Street as a place in which to congregate (see colour p.81).

ASDA 1976–7, Cockburn Associates
Extensive two- and three-storey development on site of former Aitken's Brewery, comprising shopping, offices and parking. In concrete block, its shallow pitched roof, articulated by projecting division walls, provides canopy for shoppers in High Street.

Wellington Statue, 1854, Robert Forrest
Freestone with ashlar plinth. The Lanarkshire sculptor made a strange choice of hero for a Scottish burgh! It appears that Provost Adam, an admirer of the sculptor's work, bought the 'Iron Duke' for £130 at an exhibition at Edinburgh's Calton Hill. Erected initially at the Steeple, 1854, moved to Newmarket Street, 1905.

South African War Memorial, 1905, W G Stevenson
In bronze, depicts kilted soldier standing guard over body of wounded comrade. Unveiled by Field Marshal Earl Roberts, 19 October 1906.

11 **Registrar's Office** (former Burgh Buildings), 1879, William Black
Punchy Scots Baronial cornerpiece in chunky stonework, distinguished by low-slung oriel bay supported on squat flowering column, quatrefoil and cinquefoil windows in pediments, filigree ironwork crown to truncated pyramid roof. On Glebe Street frontage, plaque with burgh motto *Touch Ane, Touch All* and sculpture of old burgh coat of arms depicting the *Bairns of Falkirk.*

Jaques

Below from top *Christian Institute; 22-23 Newmarket Street; St Andrew's Church of Scotland; Royal Bank Buildings.*

Town Hall, 1879, William Black (demolished 1968)
Lively and rhythmical composition of arched
windows with central clock tower, ogee-domed
roof and iron crown cupola.

Christian Institute, 1880–1, James Deas Page
Bold pediment, containing sculptural 'Shields of
the Institute', over Romanesque two-storey
frontage, channelled stonework and pilasters. In
the frieze, three portrait heads of worthies, one
heavily bearded – surely John Knox.

Nos 22-23, excellent four-bay composition of
triple windows, pilasters and stringcourses, all
doing the right thing at the right place. **Nos 44-
46**, fine shopfronts with egg-and-dart trimmed
fascias, **No 46**, Kynoch's, with umbrella shop
sign, a favourite Falkirk trysting place.

12 **St Andrew's Church of Scotland**, 1894–6,
James Strang
Soaring edifice in red rubble, in contrast to grey
stone of adjacent parish church, juxtaposes little
and large gothic gables flanking tall tower with
belfry and spire. Note 'Burning Bush' **sculpture**
above entrance. Built as Free Church on part of
parish church manse gardens.

Royal Bank Buildings, Nos 25-29, 1862,
David MacGibbon
Interesting but restless Scots Baronial
composition, for the National Bank, with all the
trappings – crowsteps, pedimented dormers and
turretlets. Corner porch has sculpted St Andrew
and flanking finials. The style is not surprising,
David MacGibbon together with Thomas Ross
being the authors of *The Castellated and Domestic
Architecture of Scotland*.

Above *Tudor House*. Right *Cannon Cinema*.

Falkirk Museums

Princes Street, from 1933, was opened by the Prince of Wales, later the Duke of Windsor, hence the name.

Tudor House, Princes Street, 1933
Totally inappropriate English Tudor insert presenting five friendly and well-proportioned half-timbered gables to the corner at this important junction.

Susan Skinner

Cannon Cinema, 1933, McNair & Elder
In white cement render relieved by wide bands of red brick, curved auditorium frontage flanked by Egyptian-style entrance foyers. Excellent piece of design from that optimistic period; its future currently under discussion.

Below *College of Technology*. Middle *Orchard Hotel*. Bottom *Falkirk Baptist Church*.

Jaques

13 **Community Education Centre**, Park Street, 1845–6, John Tait
Two-storey seven-bay classical former Grammar and Parochial School, under piended pavilion roof with twin central chimneys, and advanced single-storey centre. Additions, 1868, Alexander Black.

Jaques

Orchard Hotel, 2 Kerse Lane, early 19th century
Smart two-storey hostelry with painted quoins and window surrounds, rosettes at window angles, giant fluted angle pilasters and Doric doorpiece.

14 **Falkirk Baptist Church**, Orchard Street, 1897, G Deas Page
Homely T-plan in brown Locharbriggs sandstone with pinnacled gable, its neatly scaled and projecting porch protected by griffin gargoyles.

Jaques

Vicar Street
Vicar Chambers, 1903, Alex Cullen
Vigorous and determinedly asymmetrical former Grand Theatre in grey ashlar focusing on two high wallhead chimneys and robustly domed

tower recessed behind frontage. Painted ship **panel** above arched and hoodmoulded entrance.

Nos 24-28, *c.*1870
Italian astylar treatment of the whole block with its two-window end pavilions a typical mark of Peddie & Kinnear.

15 **Bank of Scotland**, Nos 39-43, 1899,
Sir George Washington Browne
Fine asymmetrical composition in red ashlar with mullioned ranks of windows, incorporating decorative carved panels under steeply pitched pediment between obelisk finials.

Left *Bank of Scotland and Old Post Office.*
Top *Vicar Chambers.* Above *Old Post Office and extension.*

Old Post Office, Nos 45-47, 1893, W T Oldrieve
Delightful gothic fancy in grey ashlar, details invariably exquisite including lacy balustrading, shallow projecting bay under central gable, corbelled angle oriel with fanciful crowning feature of mini flying buttresses. This and the bank are the jewels in this part of Falkirk's crown.
   Extension, 1970s, for Department of Employment, more than competent office block fronting Weir Street, four storeys of buff brick and slate with strongly modelled recessed balcony at third floor.

Hope Street
Former gathering place for strolling players and travelling circuses, now, part of one-way traffic system circus. Consequently, church and library are marooned in a cul-de-sac.

16 **Old Sheriff Court**, 1868–70,
Thomas Brown, Brown & Wardrop
Scots Jacobean, two storey, rubble, now Voluntary Resources Centre, with crowstepped

Above *Doorway Old Sheriff Court.*
Right *Old Sheriff Court c.1906.*

gables and projecting towers; previously included oriel-windowed **police station** and enclosed courtyard with railings and gates, making more meaningful group. Within, handsome hammerbeam roof to courtroom.

Gentleman Fountain, 1871 (demolished 1923) Formerly at prominent position outside Sheriff Court at junction of High Street and Hope Street to ease traffic congestion. Ornate iron structure with domed top, erected by Patrick Gentleman with money from his draper brother Bailie John Gentleman.

Below *Saint Francis Xavier RC Church.*
Bottom *Falkirk Public Library.*

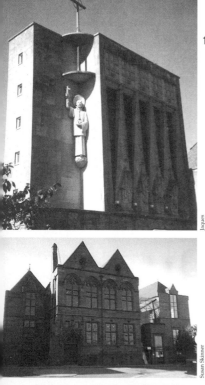

17 **Saint Francis Xavier RC Church**, 1960, A R Conlon Conventional hall fronted by tall, powerful concrete tower with stained-glass windows and latticed belfry, replacing William Stirling II's 1843 church, badly damaged in fire, 1955. In south-east angle, 12ft high Saint Francis, in Blaxter stone by Maxwell Allan. At base of massive tapered concrete supporting ribs, 'The Four Evangelists', in concrete, by Mrs Dempster. Long low stone porch with wide entrance doorway and coat of arms of Most Revd Gordon Joseph Gray by Hew Lorimer. Within 'The Stations of the Cross', on laminated glass panels by Felix McCulloch. **Presbytery**, 1902, James Strang.

Falkirk Public Library, 1901, McArthy & Watson Gothic building of some distinction in rich red-brown ashlar, with latticed windows, four bays and twin gables with quatrefoil traceried bullseye windows. Off-centre doorpiece, richly decorated and inscribed in the tympanum: *Let there be light* and *tangite unum, tangite omnes* (Falkirk's motto, see p.20). Excellent details within, including linenfold panelling. Costing £6,000, built with Carnegie grant and opened by the philanthropist himself. **Extension**, 1992, Falkirk District Council

Architects, outstanding, award-winning block in matching reconstituted stone incorporating new gable and stair in canted glass link, under deeply projecting roof.

18 West Bridge Street

Police Station, *c*.1895, William Black,
A & W Black
Well-proportioned two-storey L-plan renaissance former County Buildings, pilastered and balustraded, with Corinthian entrance porch. Keystoned oculus in generous florally decorated pediment. Under threat of demolition.

19 West Church, 1799, Thomas Stirling

Simple, large gabled rectangle with semicircular arched windows, built as Relief Church. Forebuilding, 1884, James Boucher. Giant Ionic pilasters support obelisk-crowned pediment, keystone to cavernous doorway sports crowned and bearded head of King David. Within, horseshoe gallery on cast-iron columns, Victorian furnishings and organ case. **Garden of Remembrance**, 1972, tranquil, secluded former burial ground of the Relief Church.

Philps of Falkirk Garage, 1930s, J G Callender
Well-maintained concrete and glass showroom, symmetrical with capsule decoration to centre bay. Demolition anticipated 2001. From that confident period and the same architect, curving two-storey **corner block** with horizontal banding, original fenestration, at the junction with Cockburn Street.

3 Chapel Lane

Five-bay, two-storey classical villa approached by cobbled and setted Chapel Lane, entered from homely two-storey terracing remaining from when Tanners Brae continued into High Street.

Left Police Station. *Top* Falkirk Public Library extension. *Middle* West UP (Peoples) Church. *Above* Corner block at West Bridge Street and Cockburn Street.

Cockburn Street, named after Provost Macolm Cockburn, was formed in 1927 to give an easy access to the south from the west end of the town by way of Tanners Brae and the Howgate. Previously the High Street stretched in an unbroken line to Chapel Lane and the West Church. The Howgate was a low-lying area at one time known and avoided because of its filth and squalor.

Right *Town Hall and Municipal Buildings.*
Top *Council Chambers.* Above *Westbank* .

20 **Municipal Buildings**, 1965, Baron Bercott
Well-sited and impressively relaxed group
comprising offices, town hall, district court and
health department on site of former Westbank
House. Centrepiece is handsome **Town Hall**, in
panel and curtain-wall construction. As
backdrop, **office block**, three storeys of metal and
glass over stone base, its flat roofscape of
assorted services massing up in nautical manner.
Six bright red municipal lamp-posts at entrance
provide the appropriate touch of civic pomp.
Council Chamber, monopitch single storey,
perched somewhat precariously on banking to
east. **Westbank**, health centre, 1959, A J N Currell,
sports impressive semi-glazed gable, flanking
panels enlivened by gridded design.

The First Battle of Falkirk, 22 July 1298
Grahamston is traditionally known as
the site of the battle between the forces
of Edward I of England, the 'Hammer of
the Scots', and the Scots, led by William
Wallace. Overpowered by superior
numbers, the Scots retreated, and
crossing the Carron, marched
northwards. It was in this battle that Sir
John Graeme of Dundaff and Sir John
Stewart of Bonkhill were killed, their
gravestones to be seen in Falkirk
churchyard (see p.11).

Grahamston Station.

Grahamston
The twin successes of the Carron Iron Company,
1759, and Falkirk Iron Works, 1810, were
principally responsible for the years of Falkirk's
prosperity. With this went the huge expansion of
the town, particularly north to Grahamston,
Bainsford and Carron itself. Architecturally, one
finds workers' housing, small-scale Georgian and
Victorian opulence side by side.

21 **Grahamston Station**, 1986, F J McCracken
Lower of Falkirk's two stations, crisply designed
flight of fancy for ScotRail, planned and entered
on the diagonal with dominant barrel rooflight,
deep fascia and red trim.

Graham's Road
Stretch of handsome small-scale Georgian houses,
rapidly being eroded by modern building and
traffic developments, includes **Nos 4-6**, early 19th
century, single-storey with Doric doorpieces and –
for confusion's sake – Tudor hoodmouldings.

Nos 58 & 60, *c*.1840
Two houses with Tudor motifs, Greek Doric
columned centre door, raised steps and full
basement; No 58 converted to office.

Institute of Foundry Workers, 1890 (demolished)
Victorian confidence exemplified in expansive
lettered frieze, decorative entrance panel and
pilastered doorpiece.

Graeme Hotel
Yet more Victorian exuberance, three storeys with
pedimented dormer and florid baroque doorpiece.

Graham's Road Church, 1878, A Watt
(demolished)
Gaunt gothic pile with octagonal corner tower,
slender spire rising above splayed base replaced by
reasonably well-crafted three-storey **tenemental
block** with shops below, 1995–6, Donald Macleod.

Grahamston United Church of Scotland,
Bute Street, 1874–5, T B McFadzean
Extensive gothic *quoad sacra* church entered at foot
of dramatic 120ft corner steeple with louvred belfry
and pinnacled pyramid roof. Smaller tower to
north links to **hall**. Design is a copy reverse of the
West Church at Alloa by Peddie & Kinnear (see
Clackmannan and The Ochils in this series).
McFadzean was Peddie & Kinnear's clerk of works
in the early 1860s.

Oddfellows Hall, 1883, J Strang
Self-confident pedimented and balustraded block
with slimline two-storey circular corner bay
surveying all comers. Erected by *Loyal Sir John de
Graeme Lodge of the Independent Order of Oddfellows*.

Gateway, former Grahamston Ironworks,
Gowan Avenue, *c*.1886
Impressive cast-iron semicircular arch on

*Left Oddfellows Hall. From top 58 & 60
Graham's Road; Institute of Foundry
Workers; Graham's Road Church;
Grahamston United Church of Scotland.*

Grahamston House.

consoled corbels, pilastered pillars and rosette frieze made for Edinburgh International Exhibition of 1886. On top, decorative urns and scrolled ornament with draped flags over lion rampant – Falkirk's very own Great Gates of Kiev – to be moved to Carron Phoenix site, 2002 (see colour p.84).

Grahamston House, 1990, Central Regional Council Architectural Services
Pleasantly informal single-storey home for the elderly planned round central top-lit multipurpose area. In buff facing brick, with red roof tiles and arched acrylic entrance canopy.

Bainsford
Red Lion Inn, Bankside, *c.*1800
White render, with red window margins, two-storey staging post, long associated with the Forth & Clyde Canal, now second-hand furniture dealers' (see Union Inn p.47).

Bainsford Primary School, 1974, Central Regional Council Architectural Services
Interesting linked pavilions, in roughcast with glazed and lead-clad hoods to first-floor classrooms; the effect, a herd of browsing elephants.

Bainsford Day Centre.

Bainsford Day Centre, 1985, Central Regional Council Architectural Services
First-class postmodern essay in red brick, blue-stained timber and gently pitched corrugated metal roofing; feature gable oversailing semicircular stairtower, single-storey flanking pavilions with colourful trim.

Bottom *Dalderse Cottage.*

Dalderse Cottage (demolished 1990s)
Tantalising fragment of coach house to Abbotshaugh House, part chapel, part stable with corbelled octagonal turret over narrow Saracen doorway; stone hideaway with pepper-pot roof adjacent.

Kerse Lane and Grangemouth Road

This area, to east and north east of High Street,
has seen much of Falkirk's and Scotland's history.
Kings and their retinues on the way from
Edinburgh to Stirling on the tree-lined track that
was Callendar Road would have seen fields north
of the Callendar estate; fields later to become **The
Pikes** and **Bellsmeadow**, and the estates of
Belmont and **Rose Park** with their orchards. The
changes of 1829 included culverting the East
Burn, thus removing a natural barrier to
expansion and allowing the direct continuation of
Callendar Road into High Street.

Left *Christ Church Episcopal Church.*
Below *Apse.* Middle *St James Parish
Church.* Bottom *Victoria School.*

Christ Church Episcopal Church, Grangemouth
Road, 1863–4, Sir Robert Rowand Anderson
Beautifully crafted early pointed church with
distinctive red sandstone banding to its rubble
midriff. Buttressed gable to west, cosily scaled
apse to east, bellcote over Lady Chapel and
porch. Within, banded brick walls, tiling, timber
panelling, metal screen, 1895, by Carron Iron
Company, and modern reredos. Over all, open
timber scissor trusses, gold firmament of stars in
blue sky to apse, as in Rowand Anderson's
Portrait Gallery (see *Edinburgh* in this series).
One of the architect's first works and one of his
very best.

St James Parish Church, Thornhill Road, 1900,
G Deas Page
Handsome gothic, T-plan, Locharbriggs stone
edifice, entered by way of porch in corner tower
with red tiled spire. Impressive *c.*1970 leaded-
glass window in east gable.

Victoria School, 1901, A & W Black
Four-square classical block, central pediment and
arched first-floor windows. Now used by Falkirk
Council Library Services.

Top Falkirk College of Further and Higher Education. *Above* Falkirk Fire Station.

Monument, Victoria Park, 1912
Chunky stone with splayed base and domed top sporting heraldic lion and shield commemorates the site of the First Battle of Falkirk (1298), previously only commemorated by a pair of yew trees near Graham's Road.

Falkirk College of Further and Higher Education, Grangemouth Road, 1962, Stirling County Council Architects
Extensive, flat-roofed complex includes workshops, laboratories, classrooms and full recreational facilities. Glass and panel construction, with entrance gable to four-storey teaching block having lozenge-shaped design popularised by the Festival of Britain, 1951. One of the first comprehensive Further Education Centre in Scotland.

Falkirk Fire Station, 2000,
Falkirk Council Architects
Less high-tech than some recent new buildings of this type, smart, well-articulated and elongated exercise in concrete block with shallow-pitched metal-clad roofs.

Callendar Road
Graeme High School, 2000, The Parr Partnership
Opposite Callendar Park estate, on playing fields of old high school, handsome L-shaped educational facility for 1,200, comprising elongated three-storey teaching block in concrete block and render, with split-section metal-clad roofs and eyecatching ship's prow gables; entrance, administration, conference facilities and library to north. One of five new private finance initiative (PFI) schools in the Falkirk area, two at Larbert, the others at the Braes andBo'ness (see pp.59, 101 & 149).

The five new Falkirk schools are the first examples of a 'bundled' educational project to be completed in the UK. The subject of a competition in 1997, a special company **Class 98** was set up to provide buildings and subsequent services to Falkirk Council. Teaching services remain with the Council.

Graeme High School.

Former Graeme High School (former Falkirk
Technical School), 1932, Stirling County Council
Architects (demolished 2001)
Well-proportioned, neoclassical academy for boys
and girls in red brick with stone trimmings
formed round two large courtyards.

St Andrew's RC Primary School, 1974,
Stirling County Council Architects
Accessed from Hawley Road, interesting
cruciform group of white roughcast pavilions
with slated monopitch roofs.

Top *Former Graeme High School.*
Above *St Andrew's RC Primary School.*

In 1345, after plots against him by
Patrick de Callenter, King David II
granted the estate to Sir William
Livingston. The Livingstons were to
play an important part in Scotland's
story for the next 400 years; Sir
Alexander Livingston being in effect
Regent of Scotland after the murder of
King James I at Perth in 1436.

Callendar House, from 13th century
A veritable 'Château-sur-Forth', concealed behind
and parallel to one of the finest surviving
stretches of the Antonine Wall, this extensive pile
in its beautiful grounds was home to the
Livingstons of Callendar for almost 400 years and
to William Forbes and family who bought it in the
1780s following the failed Jacobite rising of 1715.

Concealing at west end the original 14th-century
tower house, the house extends now to highly
decorative and grandly symmetrical three-storey
frontage of some 300ft in length, topped by steeply
pitched roofscape bristling with finialed turrets,
tall grouped chimneys and ornate ironwork, the
result of intensive periods of building and
rebuilding, particularly during the 17th century.
The 19th century saw the final embellishment and
aggrandisement of what had been a large, rather
plain house with the addition of a grand staircase
and *porte-cochère* on the north, entrance front, two
double-height bay windows with linking
balustraded terrace and stairs on the garden front,
and roof and chimney changes throughout,
1869–77, Brown & Wardrop, completed as
Wardrop & Reid. A set of François 1er corner

Callendar House: Left *Unexecuted scheme
by David Hamilton, 1830;* Below *South-
west stairtower;* Bottom *South elevation.*

Grand staircase.

RCAHMS

The 5th Lord Livingston was guardian of Mary Queen of Scots who visited Callendar House throughout her life. It was while she was a child there that the Scottish leaders in 1543 tore up the Treaty of Greenwich, by which Mary was to be married to Prince Edward, son of Henry VIII. Henry, enraged at the failure of his plans to unite Scotland and England by marriage, perpetrated the Hertford Raids, the so-called **Rough Wooings**, devastating the Border country and the Port of Leith.

The 7th Lord Livingston gained royal favour and was created Earl of Linlithgow. His second son was created Earl of Callendar and acquired the lands of Callendar and Falkirk. During the Civil War he changed sides several times but the Earls of Linlithgow remained loyal to the King.

In 1651, following the defeat of the Scots at Dunbar, an English force came to Falkirk and laid siege to the House. Around 50 Royalists were killed and a number taken prisoner. The Parliamentary General Monk had the badly damaged house repaired and took up residence there for a short time. Peace came with the Restoration of King Charles II in 1660, when the Earl of Callendar returned to Falkirk. James, 4th Earl of Callendar succeeded as 5th Earl of Linlithgow in 1695 but his titles and estates were forfeited following the Battle of Sherriffmuir.

After all these vicissitudes, the estate was eventually sold to The York Building Company in 1720, although the Earl's daughter was able to rent the property from them. She was the last of the Livingstons to inhabit the House. The Estate went to auction in 1783, being bought by William 'Copperbottom' Forbes and stayed in his family until bought by Falkirk Town Council in 1962.

turrets completes the picture and testifies to the excellence of the French architectural tomes in William Forbes' library.

Inside, at first floor, contrasting styles of the **drawing room** and **dining room** are the main attractions, former, possibly by David Hamilton, but more likely by James Maitland Wardrop, distinguished by swagged doorcases and elegant frieze. Latter, by Wardrop, has elaborate chimneypiece and screen. Fine too are, at the west end, **Cromwell Stair** with painted *trompe l'oeil* ceiling of frolicking putti, 1704, attributed to Dutch artist Tideman, replicated by Edinburgh artist William Kay, and, at the east end, Hamilton's beautiful **library** of 1827–30, with trellised bronze screens and elegant wooden barrel-vaulted ceiling. Required viewing are the window of the room where, allegedly, Mary Queen of Scots stayed on her numerous visits to the house (top floor, extreme north west) and superb ground-floor **kitchen**, possibly the grandest that can be visited in Scotland.

Callendar Park

A cutting through the Antonine Wall (said to have been made for the visit of Queen Victoria in 1842, actually cut in 1680) provides a dramatic view of the house from the north. To the south and east an estate layout worthy of Capability Brown changes from formal to informal as the ground rises to Callendar Woods. Here are to be found large **boating loch** and **bird sanctuary**, elegant (?)18th-century **bridge** with segmental arch, chamfered voussoirs and chain parapets, and so-called **Dry Bridge**, early 19th century, possibly David Hamilton, single semicircular arch with curved approaches. Nearer the house, well-detailed, early 18th century, gothic **stable court**, three-stage, square plan **doocot**, 1828, **former kennel**

and **ice house**. **Park Gallery**, 2000, Falkirk
Council Architects, crisply designed conversion
of former milking shed into art gallery with
eyecatching glass entrance screen and security
shutter. Hidden in the woods, **mausoleum**,
1816, Archibald Elliot, circular with Doric
columns over rusticated podium, has
tremendous *gravitas*, despite graffiti which are
extensive and modern. Former **factor's house**,
19th century, low, two storey with basement,
three bay, with later two-storey block forming
near L-plan. **Glenbrae Lodge** and **gates**, *c.*1835,
single-storey lozenge plan, broad-eaved roof,
tapered octagonal chimney shafts.

Top left *Dry Bridge*. Top *Stable court*.
Above *Mausoleum*. Left *Former Factor's
House*.

Callendar House and estate bought by Falkirk
Town Council in 1962. Following phased
refurbishment, 1974–5, A C Wolffe at a cost of
£3.3m, house now contains Falkirk Museums
Services, History Research Centre, and temporary
and permanent exhibitions (see colour p.82).
Principal rooms and grounds open to public; guidebook

Multistorey flats, 1966, Falkirk Burgh Architects
Within the estate and profiting from established
trees and landscaping, six plain but eyecatching
14-storey blocks in framed panel and brick

Translated from the Greek inscribed on
the mausoleum are these cryptic words
from Lucan:
*Those things we mortals call our own
Are mortal too and quickly flown
But if they could forever stay
Then we from them would fly away.*

William 'Copperbottom' Forbes
earned his curious sobriquet from the
way he had made his money,
supplying the Admiralty with copper
for covering ships' hulls when it was a
new idea. Having cornered the market,
he bought the business back cheaply
when the method temporarily failed,
and sold it again to the Admiralty
when the invention was perfected.

James Maitland Wardrop, 1824–82, was
in partnership with Thomas Brown
from 1849, and Charles Reid from 1873.
The firm was responsible for many
excellent buildings in the Lothians and
elsewhere, including Wigtown County
Buildings and Town Hall, 1862 (see
Dumfries and Galloway in this series),
Linlithgow Courthouse, 1863 (see *West
Lothian* in this series) Stirling Sheriff
Court, 1874 (see *Stirling and the Trossachs*
in this series) and Falkirk Sheriff
Courthouse, 1866 (see p.23-4).

33

Above *Multistorey flats*. Right *Callendar Business Park*.

Timber Hall, 981AD
One of the best preserved hillforts in the area, 80ft long by 23ft across, on site of Callendar Business Park. Known locally as Thanes Hall and being the predecessor of Callendar House, not an unreasonable attribution. RCAHMS, *Stirlingshire*

Below *Antonine House*. Bottom *Parklands House*.

The Antonine Wall was built at the successful completion of a campaign in southern Scotland undertaken by order of Antoninus Pius probably motivated by a need for military prestige to strengthen his position as the new emperor of the Roman empire. The wall, like its predecessor built under the reign of Hadrian, would have been intended to divide the island in two.

construction on low ridge south of the line of the Antonine Wall. Similar blocks in Parkfoot and Summerford, all intelligently sited and integrating well into the general grain of the town.

Parkfoot
Glenbrae Court and **Parkfoot Court**, 1966, Falkirk Burgh Architects
Exemplary group of high flats, among trees and continuing theme set in Callendar Park; refurbished 1996. **Montfort Place**, 1964, in contrast, informal layout of single-storey semidetached villas exploiting to the full the landscape at the edge of the deep dark wood.

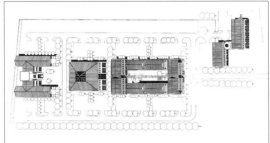

Callendar Business Park, 1992, Jestico & Whiles
For Ithaca Estates, on sheltered site of old walled garden to Callendar House at east end of the estate previously occupied by Callendar Park College of Education, 1960s, Λ Buchanan Campbell (demolished). With parking outside the site, collegiate plan comprises two parallel rows of eight well-detailed two-storey units in white blockwork with dark brick bases and trim under shallow pitched roofs, axial layout focusing on three-storey H-plan **Antonine House**, for Inland Revenue, gables and entrance articulated with gleaming concave and convex metal-clad walls.

Parklands House, 1994,
Hurd Rolland Partnership
Planned as open courtyard overlooking Callendar Loch, extensive three-storey office, for Child Support Agency, in ashlar-faced blockwork, with strip windows, making aggressive, sometimes obsessive use of 45° angle in design of huge feature window, entrance doorway and site features.

Antonine Wall, 142 AD, Antoninus Pius
Impressive half-mile long, seven-ft deep stretch of the 38-mile long (61km) barrier consisting of turf and earthen rampart on stone foundation

THE ANTONINE WALL

RCAHMS

with wooden palisade built across the narrowest part of central Scotland from Carriden on the Forth to Old Kilpatrick on the Clyde. On a continuous scarp that borders the valley, forts attached to the south side of the rampart provided accommodation for the garrison and were linked by the Military Way, a cobbled road allowing men and supplies to travel quickly along the wall. Remains of Roman **bathhouse** with hypocaust floor for the fort in Falkirk town centre were discovered west of the park in Kemper Avenue, 1980.

The Roman Fort at Falkirk was only discovered in 1991 by Falkirk Museums Department during the redevelopment of the grounds of Rosehall House in the Pleasance. Subsequent work has shown that the Fort was built shortly before the Antonine Wall, c.142AD, and is centred on the Andrian Bowling green. An industrial annexe lay to the east.

Pleasance
From the French *Pleasaunce*, to denote gardens on the edge of town. Pleasant it is, with fine villas, terracing, commanding views and south-facing slopes.

Erskine Church, Hodge Street, 1905, A & W Black
Grey rubble, cruciform gothic perpendicular pile, named after dissenter Ebenezer Erskine, dominating its corner site. Approached by dramatic flight of steps under large five-light window. Buttressed tower with belfry, balustrades and finials. **Hall** and offices behind. Within, **memorial windows**, 1905, Stephen Adam, and 'Mary Anointing the Feet of Christ', 1937, Alexander Strachan.

Redhurst, 15 Hodge Street, 1903, (?)Thomas Copland
Colour-washed two-storey villa with accented quoins, door and window trim, among stone neighbours. Tudor gable and eyecatching keyhole porch. Similar **villa**, 42-44 Gartcows Street. One of the few works reputed to be designed by the architect (together with William Gibson) of pioneering Arts & Crafts house The Hatherley, (see p.38).

Below *Erskine Church*. Bottom *Redhurst*.

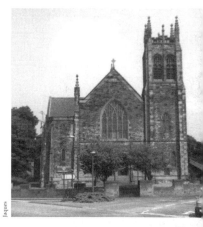

Jaques

Jaques

St Modan's Church.

Falkirk District Gymnastic Centre.

A & W Black of King's Court, Falkirk, were responsible for many of the better buildings in the area. William Black, 1840–1921, the founder's son, was responsible for a considerable body of public buildings designed with confidence and often showing real flair. Passing from baronial to classical with ease, these included the splendid Burgh Buildings, 1879, Town Hall, 1879 (now demolished), Erskine Church (see p.35) several public buildings in Grangemouth and Larbert, including the Dobbie Hall (see p.52).

Below *Woodlands*. Bottom *East block, Woodlands High School.*

St Modan's Church, Cochrane Avenue, 1914–15, Peter MacGregor Chalmers
As usual from this architect, beautifully proportioned aisled church, in rubble with ashlar surrounds. Inside, massive columns, each carved differently, support barrel-vaulted timber roof. Choir stalls, pews and pulpit in oak. Now flats, 1991, Yeoman McAllister.

Falkirk District Gymnastic Centre, St Crispin's Place, 1859, A & W Black
Well-proportioned brownstone former drill hall for Argyll and Sutherland 4th Volunteer Battalion. Note battalion's motif in pediment and handsome wide doorway.

St Crispin's Place, **Comely Place** and **Oswald Street**, *c.*1865, good Victorian stone terraces, with Masonic plaques, lead up towards the trees and high flats of Parkfoot.

Woodlands
Lying south of the old Gote Burn, Woodlands forms part of Falkirk's development over the last 150 years. Street names commemorate notable citizens such as Provost Griffiths, William Hodge and Bailie Robert Learmonth. Architecturally, a mix of styles including Victorian terracing in Hodge Street, handsome villas with iron porches in Learmonth Street and Arts & Crafts-inspired villas in Major's Place, all softened by trees and greenery of the old estates behind.

Woodlands High School (former Falkirk High School), 1898, A & W Black
Two two-storey stone blocks, east classical, west Tudor, both with many interesting details as in all the Blacks' work. Damaged by fire, demolished 2001. Replaced by Braes High School, Brightons (see p.101).

ARNOTHILL

Along a natural ridge to the west, exploited in earlier times by the Antonine Wall which drove its way across the district. The toffs have traditionally lived here; big houses and long sloping gardens in a leafy paradise.

Arnothall, 1873, T B McFadzean
Imposing, steeply gabled, bargeboarded villa, distinguished by three-stage French-roofed tower and wedge-shaped spire between projecting bays, one angled, one flat.

Eriden, 17 Arnothill, mid-19th century,
T B McFadzean
Asymmetrical two-storey villa, with Jacobean gables and strapwork parapets, mullioned and transomed windows, massive entrance porch and, exploiting the view to north, balustraded balcony between floridly decorated advanced bays. Fine timber stair with stained-glass windows and original plasterwork within. Now a nursing home. Sympathetic extension, 1990–1, G R M Kennedy & Partners.

Left *West block, Woodlands High School.*
Top *Arnothall.* Above *Eriden.*

Garthill Gardens, above-average modern 'executive homes', **No 2**, a crisp composition of monopitches and swept dormers in white roughcast and slates.

Carmelite Monastery, 3 Arnothill, 1855
Turreted baronial villa, behind high stone wall, former manse for Revd Lewis Hay Irving of the Free Church of Scotland. Extended 1934, Reginald Fairlie, as convent. Chapter room added, 1955. Poultry, bee-keeping and goats provided food for the Order up to 1970s. Now printing is among many duties undertaken.

Best Western Park Hotel, 1970s, T M Miller
Concrete framed, white roughcast and panel infills to long horizontal bedroom block perched above podium of entrance, conference and dining rooms. Ripple-arched concrete roof a child of its time reminiscent of Basil Spence's work at Coventry Cathedral and Sussex College.

Lewis Hay Irving, d.1877, minister of Falkirk Free Church for some 35 years was also a celebrated social reformer and leading figure in the movement for better local government, a cleaner water supply, regular street cleaning, the provision of a poor house, a ragged school for the education of poor children and a savings bank.

37

The Hatherley: Right North front; Top South front; Above Stair detail.

Thomas Copland & William J Gibson
Just who designed what at The Hatherley will always be a mystery. Both men were qualified architects, and both did other work in the town, Gibson at the Infirmary and Copland being responsible for the Railway Hotel and houses in Hodge Street, Gartcows Road and Slamannan Road. However none of the other schemes of either men, competent though they were, show the same flair as The Hatherley. Perhaps therefore it was a marriage of inspiration as well as convenience. Only one thing is certain – Copland's name is on the drawings.

Mayfield.

The Hatherley, Arnothill Lane, 1904, Thomas Copland
Arts & Crafts gem for the architect William Gibson, who possibly had a hand in its design. Harled with stone dressings, semidetached two-storey villa with central three-storey tower (half the house was for the client's mother and aunt). Contemporary with Mackintosh's Glasgow School of Art and with similarities to James MacLaren's work in Perthshire (see *Central Glasgow* and *Perth & Kinross* in this series). **Terrace** to south, single-storey walled **office court** to rear. Inside, open stairwells, generally flowing spaces and much excellent period detail: dark-stained timber panelling, running dados at door height, inglenooks, superb door furniture and decorated ceilings, all beautifully maintained, as house and restaurant, by Gibson's granddaughter.

Arnothill Lane, cosily narrow and confined between flanking stone walls, joins Maggie Wood's Loan and dives down to Westburn Avenue and Falkirk Royal Infirmary.

Mayfield, 7 Maggie Wood's Loan, *c.*1860, Italianate two-storey bay-windowed mansion with staged tower and arcaded loggia. **Arnot Grange**, No 3, classically simple stone villa in setted courtyard, the office of Wilson & Wilson Architects.

Falkirk & District Royal Infirmary, Westburn Avenue, 1932, William J Gibson
Extensive, axially planned, mostly two-storey neoclassical pavilions in white render with hipped grey slate roofs erected on former Garcows Estate and replacing William Black's Cottage Hospital at Thornhill Road. Infirmary cost £100,000 and was opened in 1932 by HRH Prince George (later Duke of Kent). **Falkirk Ward**, Major's Loan, 1966, Keppie Henderson &

Partners, three storeys with glazed outshots containing day spaces. Pioneering block in its time, introducing four- and six-bed wards and 'race-track planning' as nursing aid.

Accident Unit, 1973, Wilson & Wilson, flat-roofed framed and glazed block neatly resolving varying levels on site – Out Patients on top, Accident and Emergency below – canopies for entrances and ambulances.

Maternity Block and **Geriatric Unit**, 1987, George Horspool & Partners, somewhat lumpy facility in dark red brickwork with service superstructure clad in lead.

Dollar Park

Arnotdale, Camelon Road, 1832
Large Victorian two-storey, ashlar mansion with consoled balconies, pediments and Doric doorpiece; remodelled 1950s. Approached by long drive and defended by two Chinese lions, all among fine estate trees, shrubs and flower beds. Garden statuary includes 'Prodigal Son' by Robert Forrest; to the rear, octagonal doocot, 1834, with ogee roof and dormer access for the doos. The house together with its gardens gifted to the town by Robert Dollar.

War Memorial, Camelon Road, 1926,
Leonard Blakey
Finely proportioned 12ft high Lutyensesque cenotaph protected by iron railings and pillars approached by shallow steps. Unveiled by the Duke of Montrose.

Kilns House, 1852, William Stirling III
Two-storey, asymmetrical, Tudor Jacobean villa, now houses Falkirk Council's Community Services Department.

Burnbrae Lodge, Kilns Road, 1890s
Smart hipped-roof lodge with projecting timber

Left *Falkirk Ward.* Top *Entrance detail, Falkirk & District Royal Infirmary.* Middle *Accident Unit.* Above *Arnotdale, 1932.*

Robert Dollar was born in Grahamston and made a fortune in America in the timber and shipping businesses, the latter involving much travel in China and the Far East. As well as gifting Dollar Park and the library in Hope Street to the town, he provided bells for the parish church and a fountain in Victoria Park commemorating Sir John de Graeme.

Robert Barr, one-time resident of Arnotdale, began production of aerated water in 1873, while keeping up his father's trade of cork-cutting. The business became so successful, that he eventually concentrated all his efforts on increasing the production of 'ginger'. Although many firms produced a similar product, Barr's recipe proved to be the most popular, becoming the trademark Irn Bru, in 1946. In early 1995 the plant at Lock 16, Tamfourhill closed, and moved to a new site at Cumbernauld, thus ending 120 years of Barr's products being bottled in the town.

porch, white render with black surrounds to round-headed windows and doorway.

Kilnside, Kilns Road, 1894, Sir J J Burnet
Handsome two-storey, L-plan villa, for manager of Camelon Iron Works, with bracketed porch in the angle, small corner turret and two adjacent two-storey bay windows to north. Fine period details within.

Darroch House
L-plan Victorian mansion with pedimented gable and balustraded porch in the angle.

Bantaskine
Former estates of Bantaskine stretched from existing slopes below Arnothill to Falkirk's wooded high ground to the south; the latter, because of its elevation, providing dramatic views across canal, railway and town to the Firth of Forth and the hills of Fife beyond.

Long since gone, **North Bantaskine House** was home to the Laird of Bantaskine who played an important part in Falkirk's early history.

Top *Burnbrae Lodge*. Middle *Kilnside*. Above *Darroch House*.

The Laird of Bantaskine also had substantial lodgings in the High Street and figures prominently in the 17th-century history of the area. Bantaskine itself is recorded for many centuries, as was Bantaskine Port, a main point of entry to the High Street from the south. According to the *Second Statistical Account* of 1845: *Bantaskine House, the residence of T C Haggart Esq is an elegant and substantial mansion of modern architecture. It stands on an elevated spot, half a mile south west of the town, and partakes of the fine prospect ... the grounds are encircled by luxuriant plantations.*

The Development of South Bantaskine
In 1844 I rebuilt and have since enlarged the Mill in Valleybank and put into it two hundred power looms, and this factory is carried on under lease from my cousins in Kilsyth. In 1846 I purchased a property in Grahamston for £235. [In] 1848 I purchased an old property on the High Street of Falkirk [Wilson's Buildings, see p.16] on which I erected a large building which with the purchase money cost me about £7,000... In June of the same year I resolved to take to myself a wife and selected Mary Russel as the object of my affections.
Alistair Campbell, from 'Notes on his Life' by John Wilson, Coalmaster, Calatria No 6

South Bantaskine House, 1860 (demolished 1950s)
Built by John Wilson, coalmaster, to accommodate his wife and eight daughters, or, as he put it *forty feet of daughters*. Of the mansion and grounds, only **walled garden** and **gates** remain as part of public park. **Stained glass** from main stair of house, depicting Charles Edward Stuart and his generals, now in Howgate Shopping Centre (see colour p.81).

Bantaskine Boat House, 1991, Ross Smith and Jamieson (*below*)
Cheerful little facility in crisp buff brick, for Seagull Trust, with blue engineering brick trim to windows and quoins, three distinctive tall, arched and dormered windows, in beautiful setting on the canal (see colour p.82).

Union Canal Tunnel.

The passengers on their way from Edinburgh, will have seen with surprise, the aqueducts, and other various works, which have been constructed on the line of this canal; but when here, they see the wide chasm, and the distant light, glimmering through the lonely dark arch of nearly half a mile in length, they are struck with feelings of awe; and as they proceed through it, and see the damp roof above their heads - feel the chill rarefied air - and hear every sound re-echoing through the gloomy cavern - their feelings are wound to the highest pitch. At the same time there is something uncommon and interesting in the idea that, there, secluded from the light of day, they are silently gliding through the bosom of a hill, whose surface is cheered by the enlivening rays of the sun, and covered with crops, cattle and the cheerful dwellings of man.
John Aitken, *A Companion for Canal Passengers betwixt Edinburgh and Glasgow*, 1823, as quoted in *Calatria No 11*

Union Canal Tunnel, Prospect Hill, 1818–22, Hugh Baird
Rock-cut, 600m long, faced with masonry and brickwork, simple arches at each end set in concave retaining walls of rough ashlar. William Forbes refused to allow the canal to pass within sight of Callendar House, with the result that it passed by means of the only canal tunnel in Scotland.

Obelisk, Greenbank, 1927, A & W Black
Octagonal, stone, moonrocket of a monument marks centre of the site of the Second Battle of Falkirk in 1746.

Standalane Farmhouse, Lochgreen
Evocatively named single-storey farm steading with pedimented dormers; wooded background, breathing rural tranquillity.

Creve, 6 Lochgreen Road, 1930s
Sprightly villa, white walls, metal corner windows including that to stair, slimline bus-

Above *Obelisk, Greenbank*. Left *Creve*.

The Second Battle of Falkirk
In January 1746, Prince Charles Edward Stuart's Jacobite army led by Lord George Murray defeated the Hanoverian army.
Both armies were well matched in point of numbers, each consisting of some 8000 men, and the day ended in a defeat of the government troops with 29 killed and wounded. The irregular nature of the ground and other causes led to the discomfiture of Hawley; but after the Battle of Falkirk, Charles' success terminated.
Second Statistical Account, 1845

shelter type porch. One of many fine examples of houses of that period in this road.

Tredinnock, 33 Slamannan Road, 1906, Thomas Copland
Handsome half-timbered villa, windows punched out in sandstone dressings; Copland's Art Nouveau details more obvious in buttressed porch, flared chimneystacks and, within, numerous details including timber lattice work to staircase. See also The Hatherley (p.38).

Lochgreen Hospital, Slamannan Road, 1881, A & W Black
Single-storey, H-plan, symmetrical, three-bay central block surrounded by balconied pavilions looking out over trees and greenery (these now demolished). Built as fever hospital and sanatorium on high ground and distanced from the town.

Top *Tredinnock*. Above *Windsor Hospital*.

Windsor Hospital, Woodlands, 1904, William Black (demolished 1990s)
Impressive and extensive former Combination Poorhouse comprised baroque central block, well articulated but somewhat gaunt pavilions to rear all climbing the contours. Complex entered by way of arched, pedimented, single-storey gatehouse.

Right and below *Summerford House*.

Summerford House, Summerford Road, 1986, Central Regional Council Architectural Services
Doughnut-plan in warm buff brick and red tiles, glazed central court providing sympathetic accommodation for the elderly; saw-toothed perimeter exploits views while retaining privacy.

Camelon

Tradition has it that the ancient city of Camelon was a harbour on the ever-shifting River Carron as it made its way to the sea; fragments of anchors and ancient boats having been found embedded in its soil. Apart from these artefacts, no trace remains; today the sea lies many miles away.

In Roman times, a gap in the wall at Watling Lodge gave passage to the main north road. Glasgow Road and Lochlands Industrial Estate occupy the sites of former camps, that at Lochlands defending the principal crossing of the River Carron and supplying the armies stationed in the north.

The Afghan passing below Camelon Bridge c.1896.

View from High Locks c.1910.

Camelon locks.

In later days, with the coming of the canals and the railways, Camelon was to share in Falkirk's prosperity and had its own iron foundries but it was nail making, established by William Cadell, son of Carron's founder, that was the principal employment at the time of the *Second Statistical Account* of 1845. This prosperity was in large part owing to Camelon's position at the junction of the canals; 11 locks climbing 110ft joined the Forth & Clyde and Union Canals at Port Downie. Camelon, a decade ago rather drab, has recently been redeemed by a string of good buildings, although still suffers from a lack of recognisable focus. This may well be remedied with the Falkirk Wheel, part of an extensive £78m scheme by British Waterways to reinstate, upgrade and put into new use the Forth & Clyde and Union Canals.

Port Downie was named after Robert Downie of Appin, president of the canal company. Thomas Telford had suggested continuing the canal to join the Forth and Clyde at its summit at Wyndford Lock, three miles east of Kilsyth. So too did Robert Stevenson in his plan. This would have saved considerable time in navigation between Glasgow and Edinburgh, cutting out four locks on the Forth and Clyde and reduced the number joining the two canals together to seven. But it would have meant cutting at least six more miles of canal and erecting another great aqueduct at Castlecary.

Mariner Centre, Stirling Road, 1985, Falkirk District Council Architects

Mariner Centre.

44

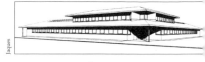

Strongly articulated leisure box enlivened with huge luminous green lettering contains free-form leisure pool, squash courts and games hall in lively and colourful interior.

Camelon Health Centre, Baird Street, 1988, Richard Jaques with Common Services Agency
Handsome elongated L-shaped block in warm red facing brick with strip windows and generous oversailing roof. Entered on the diagonal with ship's prow glazing to doctors' common room over.

John O'Hara Court, Baird Street, 1988, Wheeler & Sproson
Cosy courtyard group of single- and two-storey white roughcast flats for the physically disabled, for Margaret Blackwood Housing Association, with projecting feature windows clad in lead, neat landscaping to paviored court.

St John's Parish Church, Glasgow Road, 1838, David Rhind
Originally rectangular plan, simple and well-proportioned, advanced bay with three arched windows and bellcote at north gable. Romanesque aisle addition, 1924, Peter MacGregor Chalmers, fronting the original.

St Mary's of the Angels RC Church, Glasgow Road, 1960, Gillespie, Kidd & Coia
Flat roofed, L-shaped church and priest's house in variegated brick enlivened with decorative soldier courses. Magical interior, as is usual with this firm of architects; the clerestory bathes the balcony, natural brick walls, timber roof beams and solid pews in strong primary coloured shafts of light (see colour p.84). Art works include the sculpture 'The Woman Taken in Adultery', by Vincent Butler.

Top *Camelon Health Centre.*
Above *Camelon Church of Scotland.*

Gillespie Kidd & Coia, 1927–80
Following on from the firm's robust and eclectic pre-war work, mainly churches in the west of Scotland, the firm was joined by Isi Metzstein in 1945 and Andrew MacMillan in 1954. Continuing with church work, the firm's reputation was to blossom with such pioneering works as St Paul's, Glenrothes, 1956, St Bride's, East Kilbride, 1963 and St Peter's Seminary, Cardross, 1965, the latter perhaps the most eloquent building in Scotland of the 20th century. Student residences at Hull University, 1967 and Robinson College, Cambridge, 1980, rounded off the work of one of the most remarkable practices in the UK.

St Mary's of the Angels RC Church.

Right *Falkirk Sheriff Court.* Top *Link Blocks, Camelon Day Centre.* Middle *Beefeater Steak House.* Above *Rosebank Distillery.*

Further proposals for the Rosebank Distillery site by British Waterways and UDV include, as well as various linking buildings, service facilities for the resurgent canal traffic, possible re-use of warehousing for residential and museum purposes and the reinstatement of a former dry dock.

Irving Parish Church of Scotland.

Falkirk Sheriff Court, Glasgow Road, 1990, RMJM
Symmetrical flat-roofed justiciary in finely bonded ashlar, entered under projecting semicircular bay, set back from road and slightly pompous with it. Houses three courts, two jury, one non-jury, all on first floor. Within and without high-quality finishes meticulously detailed, including marble entrance hall and oak-panelled court rooms.

Link Blocks, Camelon Day Centre,
Glasgow Road, 1990s, Central Regional Council Architectural Services
Two lively single-storey blocks with stepped and gridded window features under broad pediments.

Beefeater Steak House, Camelon Road, 1864, R W Rankine
Landmark warehouse of former Rosebank Distillery, probably founded 1817 by James Robertson, with curved brick end wall, separated by the road from its distillery with lofty brick chimney and further warehousing; huge iron-banded timber vats now gone. Canalscape is particularly eloquent here, almost Dutch, with good views north and south and fine walks along the towpaths and by way of the public parks (see colour p.83).

Irving Parish Church of Scotland, Dorrator Road, 1889, George Deas Page
Simple stone gothic structure with belfry over large three-light window, central rose and entrance below.

Canal Inn, Lock 16, Canal Street, *c*.1800
Two-storey howff in white render with black trim for canal users and workers.

Left *Union Inn*. Above *Canal Inn*.

Union Inn, Tamfourhill Road, Port Downie,
Lock 16, early 19th century
Three-storey waterside hostelry, ashlar with
rusticated ground floor, margined windows and
quoins, semicircular stairtower and courtyard
to rear, hugely popular as changeover point
during canal's heyday. Known to locals as
'Auntie Kate's'.

Watling Lodge, Antonine Wall, Tamfourhill,
142 AD, Antoninus Pius
Set on edge of north-facing scarp, perhaps the
most impressive stretch of the 40ft wide and
12ft deep V-shaped ditch and rampart to
survive. Gateway nearby controlled the
crossing of the wall by the main Roman road
north to Ardoch (Braco) and Strathearn (see
colour p.83).

22 **Falkirk Wheel**, Carmuirs, completion 2001,
RMJM with Kenneth Grubb Associates Engineers
Scotland's answer to the London Eye, based on
an originating idea by Nicoll Russell Architects,
is the centrepiece of British Waterway's £78m
Millennium Link project to reunite the Forth &
Clyde and Union Canals. The wheel complex,
115ft high (equivalent to a nine-storey block of
flats) and 100ft long, will lift boats and people
from one canal to the other, replacing the former
flight of 11 locks. Capable of lifting eight boats
weighing up to 600 tons in 15 minutes, it will be
the first rotating boat lift in the world (see p.5
and colour p.83).

HALLGLEN
Hallglen and Glen Village occupy a privileged site
south of Callendar Wood in the lovely valley of the
Westquarter Burn, Glen Village, a former mining
community, being tucked in low beside the canal.

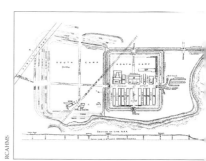

Camelon Roman Fort.

*Before we go into Falkirk, we crossed the
famous canal which connects the waters of
the Atlantic with those of the German
Ocean, coming out into the Firth of Forth
and ending, as we shall by and by see, in the
Clyde between Greenock and Glasgow. The
manner in which such a thing so apparently
wonderful has been effected, neither my
taste nor my time will induce me to
endeavour to describe; it is sufficient for me
to know that the thing is, and sufficient for
the greater part of my readers to know, that
by means of this canal, goods of any weight
are much more easily sent from Greenock
and Glasgow to Edinburgh than from
London to Barnet or to Uxbridge.*
Thomas Pennant, *A Tour in Scotland in 1769*

47

Right Hallglen. Below *Hallglen Centre.*

Hallglen Housing, 1970,
Scottish Special Housing Association
In white roughcast and grey slates, this huge hillside development, for Falkirk Burgh, without any variation in form, layout or colour, is well-known to railway commuters but does little *en masse* to relieve the monotony of the journey. Closer up, it reveals its good points, many footpaths threading their way through swathes of well-kept lawns and landscaping, set against the huge green backdrop of Callendar Wood.
Meikland, lower down beside the Glen Burn, has profited by earlier mistakes, some pastel renderings varying the visual diet.

Below *Falkirk Riding Centre.* Middle *Church of Jesus Christ Latterday Saints.* Bottom *Laughing and greeting (crying) faces, Bridge No 61.*

Hallglen Centre, 1976,
Falkirk District Council Architects
Flat-roofed complex in brown brick, with deep fascias and clerestory windows, on top of exposed hillside site, with pitched roof to apse tower.
Shopping Arcade and **Snooker Centre**, in brick and roughcast, the latter with sculptural qualities that would look good given a coat of paint.

Falkirk Riding Centre, Woodend Farm, 1880
From its eyrie on the hill above, symmetrical stone single-storey farmhouse, distinguished by tall grouped chimneys and courtyard to rear.

Church of Jesus Christ Latterday Saints, 1983,
Austin Hall Constructions Ltd
Crisp evangelical exercise, on a clerical eminence, in buff and brown brick with grey slate roof. Interesting spiky tripod tower.

Woodend Walk starts here, threading its way through Hallglen estate.

Bridge No 61, Glenbrae, 1821
One of the best examples of the fixed stone bridges on the Union Canal, known as the 'laughing and greeting bridge'. It features two faces, one smiling, one frowning, said to represent two canal contractors whose respective territories met at this point.

Falkirk Museums

LARBERT

North of Falkirk and the River Carron, the adjoining villages of Larbert and Stenhousemuir enjoy a friendly rivalry. Both grew up round the railway which serviced the developing industry, Larbert Junction being an important link between the centre of the country and the ports of Glasgow and Leith.

Larbert Cross

Still very much the centre of Larbert, although road-widening schemes have inevitably reduced its former cosiness. **Red Lion Inn**, *c.*1870, three-storey hostelry overlooking the busy crossroads. Note cheerful, heavily bewhiskered **sculptural lion** on gable of brownstone opposite.

23 **Larbert Old Parish Church**, 1820, David Hamilton
Perpendicular English Gothic rectangular plan with square bell tower looming large over surrounding landscape. Replaces earlier 16th-century church rebuilt by Revd Robert Bruce of Kinnaird. Chancel added, 1911. Within, gallery on three sides. **Graveyard** contains numerous unusual cast-iron tombstones, also decorative iron **obelisk** to James Bruce of Kinnaird, 'The Abyssinian Traveller', **memorial** to Joseph Stainton of Biggarshiells and classical **mausoleum** to William Dawson, both managers at Carron Iron Company. (See p.66.)

Top *Larbert Cross c.1920*. Middle *Red Lion Inn*. Above *Sculptured lion opposite the Red Lion Inn*.

James Bruce of Kinnaird, 1730–94, was one of the most celebrated Scots of the 18th century. He gained instant fame following the publication of his travels in Africa and Egypt and in particular of his discovery of the source of the Blue Nile.

Ironically after a life spent crossing oceans and traversing continents, James Bruce was to die following a fall down the steps of his house at Kinnaird at the relatively early age of 64.

Above *Mausoleum to William Dawson.*
Right *Old Manse.*

Below *James Bruce obelisk.*
Right *Larbert Viaduct.*

Old Manse, 1635
Handsome two-storey rectangular plan, restored, 1955, in rubble and pantiles, crowsteps ending in ogival skewputts, with moulded eaves course; date lintel on north elevation.

Larbert Viaduct, 1848, Joseph Locke,
Locke & Errington, engineers
Magnificent 15 arches over River Carron, for Scottish Central Railway; in coursed rubble with dressed stone at the arches. **Larbert Mill**, *c.*1800, nostalgic survivor in white render with black window and door surrounds.

Main Street, 1901
Good Victorian brownstone terracing with two-storey projecting bay windows punctuated by corner turrets with flamboyant iron crowns. Similar terraces in **Dundarroch Street**, **Eastcroft Street** and **Pretoria Road**.

Sir John de Graeme Court, 1981, Baxter Clark and Paul
Well-handled modern housing, a pend feeding internal courtyard of two-storey cottages with bay windows.

Union Place, 1965, and **St George's Court**, 1972, Stirling County Council Architects
Two contrasting layouts demonstrating change of philosophy between 1960s and '70s: former, two storeys in roughcast and slates; latter, four-storey towers in attractive landscaping.

Larbert Station, Main Street, 1976
Crisp curtain-glazed booking hall serves 350,000 passengers a year. **Station Hotel**, 1890s, like many another, Tudor in style and a familiar landmark.

Torwood Foundry, Foundry Road, early 19th century
Office and workshop of Jones & Campbell in painted brick, three-storey office having brick pilasters and capitals, large semicircular windows to workshops.

Top *Sir John de Graeme Court*. Middle *Larbert Station*. Above *Torwood Foundry*. Left *James Jones & Sons Ltd*.

James Jones & Sons Ltd, Broomage Avenue, 1930s
Red brick with stone bandings, wafer-thin concrete entrance canopy, streamlined and flat-roofed head office for well-known timber merchants.

Well known throughout Scotland, James Jones' timber business was founded in 1875 by Mr Tom Jones with a small yard at Camelon, and soon moved to Larbert. One of their customers was Captain Scott of the Antarctic whose ship, the *Discovery*, was built with timber from Jones' yard. By the 1950s and '60s there were 40 Jones sawmills around the country and Jones had become one of the biggest timber merchants in Britain. Torwoodhall was the family home.

South Broomage
An area that has it all, particularly Carronvale Road; Victorian cottages, villas and mansions, some excellent 1930s' houses and two fine Victorian mansions, Woodcroft and Carronvale House.

Carronvale Road
Torwoodhall, 1850s
Haughty polygonal lantern crowns large L-plan gabled and bay-windowed villa surrounded by huge trees, former home of James Jones, timber merchant. **Beechmount**, another L-plan bay-windowed villa, former home of Major Robert Dobbie, now converted to flats and surrounded by three 'executive' villas in its grounds.

Torwoodhall.

Woodcroft, 1888, T L Watson
Huge broad-shouldered asymmetrical English Arts & Crafts mansion for George Sherriff. Deep-

Woodcroft.

Right Stair hall, Carronvale House.
Below Carronvale House.

eaved red tiled roof, rubble walls with ashlar dressings and dramatically projecting bargeboarded gables. Vacant and decaying; new house in garden.

Carronvale House, 1896, Sir J J Burnet
Two-storey, deep plan round small internal court, beautifully proportioned, first-class remodelling of 18th-century house, for George Sherriff. Harled with ashlar dressings and shallow-pitched red-tile pavilion roof oversailing two bay windows in mature gardens overlooking the Carron. Within, rich Jamaican mahogany panelling in stair hall, deep plaster frieze in sitting room, stained-glass panels of castles in main front rooms. Now Boys' Brigade Headquarters, with modern additions to rear. Elegant tile-hung **lodge**.

Ryedale, 1890s
Charming white-rendered Gothick lodge with black door and window trim.

Below Larbert West Church of Scotland.
Bottom Whitewalls.

Larbert West Church of Scotland,
Burnhead Brae, 1901, J P Goodsir
Presents two gothic gables to road, on precarious undulating site, to east that of the church hall, 1898, to west that of the church, 1901, latter, L-plan with projecting stairtower, built when hall was found to be too small for services.

Whitewalls, Main Street, 1930s
One of a group of Persil-white children of the time with original steel windows but added roofs.

Dobbie Hall, Main Street, 1900, A & W Black
Macho six-bay ashlar hall, built for £10,000, with hipped slate roof, set behind exuberant if heavy baroque front. Inside, U-shaped gallery, richly decorated coffered ceiling. Two-storey stage block behind. Erected to commemorate the ending of the war in South Africa, a 1900 edition of the *Falkirk Mail* stated: *Not any or all of the South*

Dobbie Hall.

Major Robert Dobbie, 1840–1908, founder of Dobbie, Forbes and Company, and donor of the Dobbie Hall, was born in Alloa and worked in Camelon Foundry as a boy, eventually becoming manager at Smith & Wellstood's works in Bonnybridge. He lived at Beechmount, Carronvale Road (see p.51).

African victories could have been celebrated in a more tangible form. In front, **war memorial**, 1922, George Washington Browne with J J & P McLachlan, sculptors, cenotaph incorporating bronze wreaths and plaques to the fallen. Original elegant lamps and railings of the Blacks' design have gone.

WEST LARBERT
Royal Scottish National Hospital (West)
Larbert Colony Extension, 1936, James Miller Curve of five balconied pavilions flank central battlemented administration unit. Original facilities included workshops for boys, workrooms for girls, laundry, recreation hall, farm and vegetable gardens. Not exactly the modern idea of care in the community, but a visionary approach to mental healthcare that for its time was truly remarkable and one implemented with all the confidence of those times.

Left *Larbert Colony pavilion.* Below *Administration Block, Larbert Colony.* Bottom *Colony Hospital, 1937, James Miller, crisp white cubist-style, second-floor balconies for tuberculosis sufferers.*

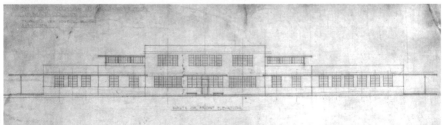

Royal Scottish National Hospital complex.

Larbert House, 1822, David Hamilton
Elegantly classical house for Sir Gilbert Stirling
with two shallow curved bays to main frontage,
overlaid with many Victorian additions
including lower balustraded west wing with
ornate tower, curved linking loggia and *porte
cochère*. House overlooks a pond, a popular
venue for curling in those days when *the roarin'
game was played outside*. Derelict **stables**, also
David Hamilton, plain but dignified symmetrical
courtyard block entered through tall archway
under central pediment.

Larbert House.

Frederick Thomas Pilkington, 1832–98,
was a Lincolnshire man, with an
architect and Methodist father. He
studied mathematics at Edinburgh
University and became an architect.
Appointed as architect to Royal Scottish
National Hospital on strength of
winning competitions for Trinity Free
Church at Irvine and the Barclay
Church at Bruntsfield, Edinburgh (see
Ayrshire and Arran and *Edinburgh* in this
series). His trademarks, flamboyantly
confident, formalistic invention
counterpointed by sculptural ornament
of great delicacy – a Beethoven of the
architectural art.

24 **NORTH LARBERT**
**Royal Scottish National Hospital
Administration** and **Skye Blocks**, Bellsdyke Road,
1862, Frederick Thomas Pilkington
East site cornerstone buildings with superb
architectural invention and floral sculptural
ornamentation, sole survivors of pioneering
mental health complex. Hugely characterful
French Gothic, chunky two-storey

Administration Block.

Administration Block, with piended roof, bracketed eaves and arcaded belfry, advanced centre bay upon beefy Romanesque loggia with splayed buttress legs taken up to support round-headed first-floor arches, framing scalloped gothic windows. Subtle layering of façades as well as exuberant decoration makes Pilkington's work instantly recognisable and memorable. Flanking the entrance, two contrasting bays. At roof level, two huge, battered and pierced chimneystacks and crowstepped wallhead chimney, both having linking coping stones, another Pilkington trademark. **Skye Block**, behind, with arcading, a comforting feature in the Scottish climate, its stumpy columns having robust sculptural stonework contrasting with delicate floral and animal capitals including one of a mother bird feeding her young. Additions 1864–70. Boundary wall with thistle-headed railings and gablet-coped **gatepiers**.

Whether such exotic blooms were appropriate for this cause is now beside the point, but these remarkable buildings must be retained as a unique contribution to Scotland's architectural heritage, despite all pressures to make way for Central Business Park.

Bellsdyke Hospital, 1866, William Stirling III and James Brown
Generous axial layout of former Stirling District Lunatic Asylum with tree-lined avenue linking widely spaced Victorian buildings, in various styles and shapes, for a tender price of £20,000 for original hospital. Later alterations, extensions and additions, A & W Black.

Below and bottom *Carvings on Administration and Skye Blocks.*

Administration Block, symmetrical with two Italianate towers. **Succursal Block**, two storeys, grandly pedimented and scrolled, almost Vanbrugh-like in its hauteur. **Nurses Home**, 1907, huge three-storey block, in harl with Dutch gables to three advanced bays. Demolished 2001; only 'Block C' remains. Single-storey asymmetrical ashlar with bracketed skewputts.

Accommodation for the Elderly, 1998, Sir Norman Foster & Partners
Semicircular blocks for multiple occupancy by contemporary wizard of the high-tech, like a visitation from outer space. Each in risband blockwork with strip windows and barrel-vaulted metal roof. With no corridors, plan articulates into groups of individual rooms with their own dayrooms, these facing onto central landscaped courtyard (see colour p.84).

Barbara Davidson Pottery, Muirhall Road, 19th century
Pleasant whitewashed traditional courtyard group, successful conversion of old Muirhall Farm for business purposes.

Middle and right Accommodation for the Elderly: Roof light; Common room. Above Barbara Davidson Pottery.

Having originated at Redding Muir, 1707–70s, the Trysts moved to Rough Castle before being held at Stenhousemuir from 1785–1900s. In a country where mountains, river and sea and the absence of roads divided the country into isolated regions, the local market was an essential part of commercial life, while larger markets were needed at central points nearer more heavily populated areas. The name *Tryst* arose from the agreements of merchant and customer and for cattle dealers who *trysted* the owners of beasts to meet them at an agreed place for the sale of their cattle. In 1727 there were 550 markets of varying sizes throughout Scotland.

STENHOUSEMUIR
Known today throughout Britain by football fans, Stenhousemuir was from 1785 to the early 1900s the third and last site for the Trysts, the huge horse, cattle and sheep fairs held on the open ground three times a year. Animals were driven from all over the country to the Trysts, which, as the biggest in Scotland, also attracted strolling performers and travelling showmen. The 1850s saw a rapid change, the railways, the steamships and the coming of the professional auctioneer, combined with changes in agricultural methods, soon robbed the Trysts of their former glory. Considerably reduced in size, the site of the Trysts exists today as the grounds of the Tryst Golf Club, Stenhousemuir Cricket Club and Recreation Ground.

Main Street
Our Lady of Lourdes & St Bernadette RC Church, 1934

Modest roughcast, slated building set back from the road. **Priest's House**, 1936, Reginald Fairlie. **Health Centre**, 1968, Stirling County Council Architects, cocky block with projecting canted cabins of dental surgeries at first floor. **Plough Hotel**, early 19th century, three-storey dormered landmark in white-and-black livery on gushet site commanding the approaches. **Cannon Shopping Centre**, 1980, Wheeler & Sproson, well-articulated, three-storey monopitched terrace comprising two storeys of housing over shopping arcade; carronades in the granite-setted and pedestrianised forecourt have not, alas, deterred the vandals.

Above *Plough Hotel.* Left *Cannon Shopping Centre.* Below *Stenhousemuir Equitable Cooperative Society Ltd.* Middle *Adam Grossart Court Housing.* Bottom *Larbert East Church.*

In the latter part of the day when the Tryst was over, to see every spot not only of the flat muir but of the beautifully undulated ground above, covered with cattle asleep and herdsmen in their traditional Scottish dress, either stretched in their plaids or resting for a while their wearied limbs – but still watchful – or gathered in groups and telling of the occurrences and bargains of the day – this is a scene which the agriculturalist will not soon forget and to which no one can be insensible.
The Stirling Journal, 27 Sept 1844

Stenhousemuir Equitable Cooperative Society Ltd, King Street, 1889, contains ingenious pedimented cornerpiece (original clock now removed), Masonic handshake motif in shallow pediment over door. **Adam Grossart Court Housing**, 1980, McAllister Armstrong, courtyard group in buff roughcast, stained timber projecting bays and adjacent modernist block at 113-133 King Street.

Public Library, 1972, Stirling County Council Architects, single-storey flat-roofed block with metal columns and deep fascia. **Housing & Finance Centre**, 1987, Falkirk District Council Architects, pitched roof and minuscule clock in large blue-stained timber entrance pediment. **Larbert East Church**, 1897–1900, James Strang, rubble gothic pile for Free church, with buttressed corner tower and belfry. Original fittings inside. Single-storey Arts & Crafts church **hall**, 1923, to rear.

With the aim of supplementing her husband's earnings as an aerated-water salesman in the 1930s, Mrs McGowan began to sell toffee from the window of her house in Stenhousemuir. It soon proved to be more popular than the lemonade and the family went full time into its production. Together Andrew and his son Robert turned Highland Cream Toffee and the famous cow into a huge national institution, establishing a factory in the Tryst Road where it continues today.

Above *Stenhousemuir Parish School.* Right and below *Stenhouse & Carron Parish Church.*

In August 1787 **Robert Burns** and William Nicol, a classical master at the Royal High School in Edinburgh, passed through Falkirk on their way to a tour of the Highlands. After they had visited Falkirk and its churchyard they went to the Carron Iron Company but were refused entry because it was a Sunday. Annoyed at this treatment Burns wrote (on the window of the Carron Inn) the following poem:

We cam na here to view your warks,
In hopes to be mair wise,
But only, lest we gang to Hell,
It may be no surprise:
But when we tirl'd at your door,
Your porter dought na hear us;
Sae may, shou'd we to Hell's yetts come,
Your billy Satan sair us!

Brian Watters, *Calatria No 12*

McGowan's Office and **Factory**, 1940s, Tryst Road
Well-proportioned block, boldly facetted windows, dark slate cladding, for makers of the well-known toffee. Note famous Highland Cow confectionary logo on entrance fascia.

Stenhousemuir Parish School, Muirhead Road and King Street, 1814 and 1886
Two-storey domestic building, 1814, at one time distinguished by group of monkey puzzle trees and interesting single-storey block of 1886 with tall church-like windows flanking advance feature doorway with oculus and belfry, survivors of the town's early education provision.

Stenhouse & Carron Parish Church (former Maclaren Memorial Church), 1900, Sir J J Burnet Harled, with red ashlar dressings and quoins, bold squat tower, corbelled parapet, bartizans and pyramid roof, entry through large timber-framed porch. Within, small gallery in tower, barrel roof to nave and aisle, church furniture of real quality including silvered cast-bronze **font** by Albert Hodge and **stained glass** 'Christ in Majesty' by

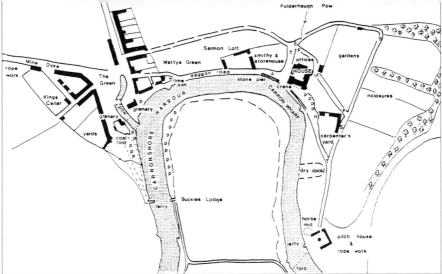

Carronshore c.1780.

Douglas Strachan. Beautifully coherent group of church, hall and two-storey, asymmetrical **manse**, 1907, with verandah, red tile roof and bargeboards, overlooking trees and garden.

CARRON/CARRONSHORE
Previously part of the barony of Quarrel, created mid-15th century, and original harbour for Carron Iron Company in 1760s before Grangemouth provided that facility. Carronshore retains a curious village character with its central green and traditional housing in North Main Street; no evidence exists of the hustle and bustle that must once have enlivened its streets, although Dock Street attests to its history.

Larbert High School, Church Street, *c.*1886, A & W Black (demolished 2001)
Strong foursquare classical former Larbert Central Public School, opened by Thomas Dawson Brodie, head of the Carron Iron Company, its classrooms, taking classes of 50–150, grouped round galleried light well, boys' and girls' entrances separate under pedimented gables. **Infant Department**, 1904, A & W Black, again strictly classical. Both school populations transferred to new buildings on site nearby.

Carrongrange School and **Larbert High School**, 2000, The Parr Partnership
Elongated group comprising two educational facilities, with trees of former Carron estate as backdrop. Former, at north end, small-scale courtyard group for special needs teaching, latter to south comprising refurbishment and extension of existing L-shaped block and new teaching block, new free-form swimming pool common to

Carron Iron Company
Iron ore was readily available in Bo'ness, water for power was plentiful and coking coal was to hand in Bo'ness, Kinnaird, Carronhall and Shieldhill. Baltic timber for the charcoal (needed for smelting the higher grade pig iron) could also be imported through Carronshore. Curiously, it was English labour that was employed in the early days of Carron and the Ironworks were known as the **English Foundry**.

Below *Larbert High School*.
Bottom *Carrongrange School*.

Top *Stenhouse*. Above *Arthur's O'on*.
Right *Carron Grange House*.

Carron Iron Company
Dr John Roebuck of Sheffield,
1718–1794, scientist and mineralogist
collaborated with Samuel Garbett, a
Birmingham businessman, in refining
gold and silver. Much of their work
required sulphuric acid, and to avoid
English patent dues they set up a works
at Prestonpans. From the success of this
they, together with William Cadell,
1708–77, and his knowledge of the
geology of the Forth, decided to invest
their profits in an ironworks at Carron.
Caddell's son, William, was the first
manager, who later made a huge
success of nailmaking in Camelon.

With the specialisation of
engineering and plastics replacing cast
iron in many household items in the
1960s, the writing was on the wall for
the Carron Iron Company as originally
set up. The Engineering Department
closed in 1969 and its Mungal Foundry,
south of the River Carron, in 1976. The
Carron Iron Company closed in 1980,
but from the ashes arose, over the next
decade, Carron Phoenix, Carron Plastics
and Carron Steelyne.

both acting as visual link. In rendered blockwork
with gunmetal grey aluminium windows and
ribbed aluminium roofs. One of five PFI school
projects built by Class 98 Ltd Ballast Wiltshier
Special Projects, other schools at Falkirk, the
Braes and Bo'ness (see pp.30, 101 & 149).

Stenhouse, from 1622 (demolished *c*.1970s)
Originally tower house built by William Bruce of
Stenhouse. Enlarged 1698 and, in 1836, to
turreted U-plan with linking entrance porch by
William Burn.

Arthur's O'on (demolished 1743)
Roman beehive structure, in dressed freestone,
20ft in diameter, 20ft high, enveloped in legend, in
what were Stenhouse policies, its demolition at
that early date bewailed today as it was then.
Replica erected on roof of office at Sir John Clerk's
estate, Penicuik (see *Midlothian* in this series).

Carron Dams
Formed to provide a further 30 acres of water for
the ironworks, built on land leased from the
Stenhouse policies; now nature reserve.

Carron Grange House, 1897, possibly H E Clifford
Superbly detailed, two-storey, asymmetrical
mansion, built for the manager of Carron Iron
Company, on wooded eminence overlooking
Carron Dams and now surrounded by sea of
'executive' homes. In pinkish rubble with tawny
brown ashlar quoins, dressings and bandings. To
west, handsome two-storey bay balanced by
corbelled and sculpted balcony. Lower kitchen
wing at north east with delightful Mackintosh-style
porch. Unequal window sashes, coloured glass to
stair well and tall chimneys crowned by delicately
corniced caps. Fine proportions and impeccable

detailing make this more than a local treasure. Semidetached **lodge**, with bracketed porches and decorative roof ridges, clearly by the same hand.

The most famous of Carron Iron Company's products were undoubtedly the **carronades**, the small naval guns used to great effect in the Napoleonic wars at the end of the 18th and beginning of the 19th century. Measuring no more than three or four feet overall they weighed three tons. Longer howitzers were also made at Carron. As well as armaments, the works produced the standard repertoire of iron products, agricultural implements, domestic appliances, fire grates, kettles, pans, spades, hoes, boilers etc. Patternmaking for the various moulds involved became a very important part of the business. The Howarth and Adam families were often used by the Company for their designs.

Left Carron Iron Company Foundry. Below Engineering Shop, Carron Iron Company, 1901, demolished 1982.

25 **Carron Iron Company Offices**, 1876, Robert Baldie (demolished 1980s)
Last vestige of Scotland's industrial crucible, administrative offices of pioneering iron foundry, 1759–1982, brainchild of Dr John Roebuck, Samuel Garbett and William Cadell. Alas, the glory is departed – only marooned and self-conscious central clocktower housing famous **carronades** in entrance loggia remains of Baldie's extensive and symmetrical two-storey stone block with crowstepped gables flanking entrance. **Office**, 1990s, tiny adjunct with shallow domed roof.

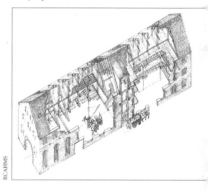

Left Carron Iron Company yard, c.1870. Below Black Mill Inn. Bottom Elon Cottage.

Black Mill Inn, between Carron and Carronshore, in white render and black surrounds, crowstepped with bullseye dormer pediments, deep cornice and pilastered doorpiece. **Elon Cottage**, 175 Carronshore Road, 1890s, inset Tuscan-pillared porch worthy of Alexander 'Greek' Thomson.

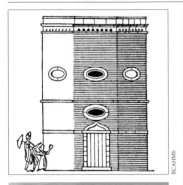

Top *Carron doocot*. Right *Carron House.*
Above *Skaithmuir Tower, early 17th
century, residence of 4th Lord Elphinstone,
in later times adapted for use as pumping
station serving coal pits of the area.
Demolished 1970s.*

Before his colossal size prevented it,
James Bruce rode round his estates on a
Clydesdale. Proud and quarrelsome, he
waged a continual one-man war against
the Carron Iron Company, whose
factories, smoke and general squalor
were, he maintained, and probably with
some justification, spoiling the amenities
and reducing the value of his estates.
Litigation with Bruce, who had briefly
trained as a lawyer, was a way of life.
Ironically, it was the wealth gained from
the sale of the coal on his estate to the
Carron Iron Company that was to finance
his years of travel abroad, without which
he would undoubtedly have had to spend
his life as a Scottish laird.

Kinnaird House.

Carron House, *c.*1770
Ruined courtyard group comprising merchant's
mansion, store block, offices and stabling in
extensive grounds by the banks of the
meandering Carron. Destroyed by fire at an early
date, traces of mansion include pedimented south
gable and arcaded loggia, wedged between
flanking wings. Later 19th-century house
incorporates bay window from original mansion.
Walled garden includes original entrance and
arcaded greenhouse structure. **Doocot,** *c.*1800,
octagonal in red brick with oval windows in each
face. **Workers' cottages,** with double-height
arched courtyard entrance and fine estate trees,
give the whole ensemble a very Gallic feel.

26 **NORTH OF FALKIRK**
Kinnaird House, 1894, James Thomson
Jacobethan mansion for Robert Orr, on site of
previous seat of the Bruces of Kinnaird, in
particular James Bruce, 'the Abyssinian
Traveller', d.1794 (see colour p.84) with *porte-
cochère*, battlemented tower with oriel and
octagonal turret. Within, impressive vaulted
hallway, grand stair and minstrels' gallery.

Two-acre **walled garden** with arched doorways and two-storey **stable block** with belfry.

Kersebrock Farm, 18th century
Whitewashed and finely proportioned two-storey, triple-dormered steading with hipped-roof porch and flanking single-storey offices, with the look of something a good deal older.

Kersebrock Farm.

Glenbervie House
Extensive Jacobean-style mansion, on site of former **Woodside House**, with dormers and ranges of grouped octagonal chimneys; in stone with red tile roof; dormered wing. **Coach house**, with central arched entrance, converted to dwelling.

*The estate of **Glenbervie**, formerly called Woodside, which includes the lands of Lethbertshiells and Stranrigmill is one of the most picturesque in the parish of Larbert.*
J C Gibson, *Lands and Lairds of Larbert and Dunipace Parishes.*

Left *Glenbervie House.* Below *Woodside House.*

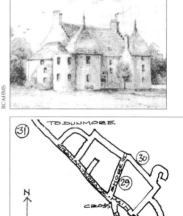

AIRTH

Today Airth has a rather downbeat appearance, its personality split between Main Street and High Street, with only latter retaining something of the quality of the old burgh. Individual buildings are of exceptional merit, reminders of Airth's considerable wealth and status as former royal dockyard, surprising since today the waters of the Firth lap a good mile away. Direct maritime links with foreign parts gave it, like Kincardine and Culross across the Forth (see *The Kingdom of Fife* in this series), a Dutch or Baltic flavour and a part of Scotland's architectural heritage that should be better known, maintained and celebrated. As it is, modern low-budget terrace infill with multicolour renderings, some stone trim and cat-slide dormers put on a brave face.

There are today virtually no traces of the Old Town of Airth, situated on the Hill of Airth, near the castle. The medieval burgh, which was founded in the reign of William the Lion, was refounded as a burgh of barony and free port on the Forth in 1597. One hundred years later, the entire community migrated to its present site, the old village finally abandoned in 1820. However, the fortunes of the new Airth were not long-lasting, it being superseded by Carronshore as port for the emerging iron industry.

Airth Castle by R W Billings.

The two hills (*ardthe* in Gaelic) of Airth and Elphinstone rise above the carselands. The hereditary family of Airth, the de Erth family, is very old and in 1240, an Adam de Erth possessed the lands of Erth, Elphinstone, Carnock and Plains. History records that from the 15th century, Edward Bruce, second son of Bruce of Clackmannan, married Agnes, one of de Erth's three daughters and thus obtained the Barony of Airth. In the 16th century the lands passed to the Elphinstones. In 1717 Graham Judge, Admiral of Scotland, acquired the estate and he and his descendents made many alterations to the castle.

Airth Castle.

William Adam scheme for Airth Castle, c.1720s–30s. A very grand affair, strictly classical and with a dominating three-bay pilastered entrance parti, it was no doubt rejected on grounds of cost.

Below *Old Parish Church.* Right *Carved figure.*

27 **Airth Castle** (now Radisson SAS Hotel), from 14th century
Originally three-storey battlemented tower house, for the Bruces of Airth, developed horizontally to L-plan, including dormer pediments with richly decorated tympana and dramatic moonrocket corner turret, rising dramatically on bluff above the Pow Burn and the flat Carselands, an impressive sight for miles around. Additions, 1803, David Hamilton, completed the triangle with three-bay two-storey symmetrical and battlemented gothic block in silver-grey stone, like a vast gateway or stage set. Estate buildings include handsome two-storey, U-shaped **stable block**, mid-18th century, repaired, William Stirling, early 19th century. **Conference centre** and three-storey **bedroom wings**, 1980s and '90s, GCA Architects, latter extending from stables to form internal landscaped court; new conservatory revitalises long-neglected formal staircase. **Old Mercat Cross**, 18th century, in castle grounds, shaft only of what may have been original town cross. **Gateway**, early 18th century, curved screen walls with balusters relocated from west approach.

Old Parish Church, late 12th century
Elegiacally romantic ruins of former parish church, reconstructed *c.*1650, abandoned 1820. Arcaded nave, with delicately carved capitals, has Airth (12th century), Elphinstone (1593) and Bruce (1614) aisles projecting like transepts, the church entered at ground floor of four-stage 17th-century tower, now, alas, without slated pyramid

roof and dormer entries for doocot. Carved slabs abound within and without, including **mortsafes**, 1830, and recumbent **figure** of veiled lady with coverlet, faithful dogs at her feet.

28 High Street
To the north, continuation of High Street climbs the contours precipitously; from top, sensational views over Carselands and the Forth to Fife and the Ochils beyond. **Mercat Cross**, 1697, octagonal shaft on stepped base, 17ft high, moulded cubic capital bearing wild boar insignia and initials of Elphinstone family, and two sundials, all crowned with acorn finial. **View Villa**, 1722, burgh style at its best, two-and-a-half storeys, steeply pitched, pantiled and crowstepped roofs. Above wide and finely moulded doorpiece, oval panel with ribbon motif, initials and date. Gable windows to attic.

Nos 46-48, early 18th century
Much altered pair, former in 1893, latter missing forestair, hence disposition of typical small windows.

Top Mercat Cross and View Villa.
Above Elphinstone Inn.

Below 5 Shore Road, now demolished.
Middle 16-18 Shore Road. Bottom
Captain's House.

Elphinstone Inn, early 19th century
Two storey in white render with black trim. Note moulded eaves course and skewputts, also shield device of wild boar, chevrons and motto *Do well let them say* – arms of the Lords Elphinstone.

Schoolhouse, Rosebank, early 19th century
Ingenious conversion of school to dwelling, including circular porch with pepper-pot roof.

Crown Hotel, early 19th century
In white render and black trim again, this time with deep cornicing and wide welcoming doorway. Opposite stood large **smithy**, with hipped roof, central doorway and pediment.

29 16-18 Shore Road, 18th century
Stone with pantiled roofs, **No 16**, two-and-a-half storeys, crowsteps and forestair; **No 18**, two storey with plain gable. Both houses with stone margins to windows and ogee-moulded eaves course.

30 Captain's House, 44 Paul Drive
Two storey, crowstepped, five windows at top, three at ground floor, a building of considerable interest, like the houses in Shore Road but here including off-centre moulded doorpiece. Note unusual lug details at ends of cornice. Three further properties, of the same quality and

Above *Airth Parish Church.*
Right *Powfoulis Hotel.*

The construction of morthouses and the making of mortsafes, massive coffins made of iron, followed the revelations about the body-snatchers and particularly Burke and Hare in Edinburgh, who at first stole buried bodies then murdered victims to sell to medical schools for use in anatomy classes. Three such found in Airth churchyard had the word Airth on the lid and the dates 1831, 1832 and 1837.

Below *Coachman's House.* Middle *Haughs of Airth, two-storey estate cottages for Powfowlis.* Bottom *Silver Link Roadhouse.*

including **The Herring House**, 1711, were demolished, 1920s.

31 **Airth Parish Church**, 1820, William Stirling English perpendicular with crocketted finials (removed) and lacy balustrading, square bell tower (with 1824 Mears bell) to north, apse to south. Spiral stair gives access to three-sided balcony. Originally located in steeply sloping graveyard, 19th-century **mortsafe** now in Museum of Scotland, Edinburgh.

32 **Powfoulis Manor Hotel**, early 19th century Charming three-storey gothic castellated confection, for James Bruce of Powfoulis, on site of earlier house, in grey ashlar and approached by double-ramped carriageway; pavilion roof, pencil-thin crocketted finials, pilasters and lacy balustrading. In entrance hall, masked head corbels support ceiling beams. Incongruous glazed and pedimented porch and two late 19th-century wings, well-intentioned but inferior quality with no crocketted finials and crude balustrading. **Coachman's House**, late 19th century, something entirely different but as fetching, crowstepped Scots Baronial, splendidly oversized corbelled corner doocot turret with pepper-pot roof, pedimented entries for the doos.

Silver Link Roadhouse, 1930s
Period piece with usual brave new world features, white walls, curved bays, Egyptian-style doorway, all under red-tiled hipped roof, latter probably replacing more traditional roof terrace. Its one-time speciality *Dancing every Sunday afternoon and evening.*

Neuck, 1812 (demolished 1970s)
Near junction of Pow Burn and River Forth, elegant late Georgian three-bay pedimented

mansion, for John Alexander Higgins, approached by elliptical double perron stair. Basement below deep cornice, attic lit by bullseye window in pediment.

Letham, late 19th century
Deep in the carselands and appearing as a mirage, whitewashed and dormered miners' cottages strung out leisurely round central green amid scattering of trees. **Letham Moss**, like Dunmore Moss to the north, very Dutch or East Anglian in character, narrow roads winding among hedgeless fields, and uninterrupted views across flat landscape. **Letham Farm**, triple-dormered farmhouse; yard, with arched, pantiled barn, opening directly off road.

Top *Neuck*. Above *Letham*.

Bruce's Castle, early 15th century
North of Airth, roofless ruin on precipitous site, some 53ft long and 33ft wide, walls generally 7ft thick. Known originally as the Tower of Carnock, it gained its present title when in the possession of the Bruces of Auchenbowie. Alexander Drummond of Carnock House purchased the castle in 1608 and kept the name of Bruce's Tower to distinguish it from the first house of the barony of Carnock.

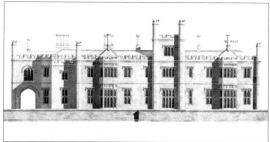

Dunmore Park.

William Wilkins, 1778–1839, was the first architect of the Greek Revival in England, his work, comprising both private houses and public buildings, culminating in the design of the National Gallery, London, in 1833. In Scotland, both in Dalmeny House, 1817 (see *Edinburgh* in this series), and in Dunmore, he was to change style from classic to Tudor, no doubt at the particular request of his clients.

DUNMORE
Dunmore Park, 1820–2, William Wilkins
Romantic ruins of extensive courtyard plan mansion, in well-wooded grounds behind meadow and ha-ha, for George, 5th Earl of Dunmore, in Tudor Gothic, entrance by way of grand *porte-cochère*. Castellations, elegant bay windows and slimline turrets abound (see colour p.84). Note magnificent avenue of lime, oak and soaring Wellingtonia. Current proposals envisage hotel with golf course. **Stable block** and **doocot**, early 19th century, gaunt battlemented gothic courtyard, cruciform arrow slits, dormer doocots over entrance arch within.

Stable block and doocot.

Elphinstone Tower and St Andrew's Church.

Below Carved seat panel, depicting 'Hope', Dunmore Chapel. Middle Dunmore East Lodge. Bottom The Pineapple and walled garden.

Elphinstone Tower, 1504
Four storeys with corbelled pepper-pot corner tower and battlemented bartizans with cannon waterspouts, erected for Sir John Elphinstone on steep slope amid lofty sequoias and elegiac yew trees; now ivy-clad ruin. Barrel-vaulted ground-floor burial place for Earls of Dunmore.

St Andrew's Church, Dunmore Chapel, 1850 (demolished)
Tiny belfried structure formed charming group with tower and terrace, with delightful views past yew trees to the Forth; only graveyard survives with flamboyant baroque **memorial** to Edward Alexander, 6th Earl of Dunmore. Surviving from chapel, five oak **panels** depicting religious events, provenance unknown but exquisite quality suggesting 16th- or 17th-century Dutch.

East Lodge, early 19th century, probably William Wilkins
Neat little building with battlemented bay window and three high octagonal chimneys.

33 **The Pineapple**, *c.*1776
Folly, for John Murray, 4th Earl of Dunmore, as birthday present for his wife Susan, daughter of 9th Duke of Hamilton, brilliant and mouth-

watering focus of six-acre brick **walled garden** and **pavilion**, 1761, set on sloping site against middle of retaining wall between flanking greenhouses or *pineries*. Huge and magnificent carving of the fruit, each leaf cantilevered out from meticulously coursed masonry (its last spiky leaf some 45ft above ground level) serves as hollow bottle-shaped roof with circular rooflight to delightful small circular chamber entered from upper level.

Accompanying ingenuities, wedding beauty to practicality, include veranda flower urns which, in connection with cavity walls, act as heating flues for the greenhouses. Restored for The Landmark Trust, 1972, Stewart Tod, Saltire Society Award for Reconstruction, 1975. (See p.5 and colour p.85.) *Owned by National Trust for Scotland; rented for holiday accommodation by The Landmark Trust*

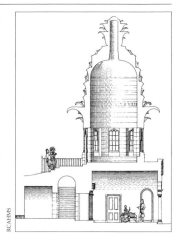

RCAHMS

Above *Section, The Pineapple.*
Left *Dunmore Model Village.*

Jaques

Dunmore Model Village, mid-19th century Stone cottages on three sides of rectangular green, for estate workers of the Earl of Dunmore, with Doric-columned and slate-roofed **drinking fountain**, on idyllic site on the banks of the Forth with views of the Ochils beyond. Cottages variously crafted in contrasting Scots and Cotswold vernacular: former with bracketed roofs, square-cut chimneys, porches and dormers; latter with clipped eaves, chamfered chimneys, slabbed gable trim and stone transomed windows. Delightful maverick **smithy**, with horseshoe doorway. **Moraig Cottage** (former schoolhouse), 1875, another excellent block with king-post brackets as gable features. See also conservation village of Muirhouses (p.153). Paternalistically conceived, these villages are redolent of a certain social equilibrium and, architecturally, of an instinctive awareness of the very best in the vernacular (see colour p.85).

Carselands (see colour p.85)
Scattered throughout the hedgeless carselands are several neat and interesting farms; **Kersie Mains**, late 17th/early 18th century, good example of small laird's house, once in possession of Earls of Dunmore, two-storey-and-

The origin of The Pineapple is shrouded in mystery. Most probably the brainchild of John Murray, 4th Earl of Dunmore, who was successively Governor of the colonies of New York and Virginia. He returned to Scotland in 1776 on the outbreak of the War of Independence and may have used part of his vast fortune to create the huge stone pineapple on the top of his earlier garden pavilion of 1761.

In the eastern colonies, the pineapple was a symbol of welcome, spiked on gateposts by plantation owners returning from the West Indies.

Below *Drinking fountain*. Bottom *Smithy.*

Falkirk Council

Jaques

69

Top *Kersie Mains*. Right *South Doll*.
Middle *South Kersie*. Above *Club's Tomb*.

basement L-plan with stair in angle. Note rolled mouldings to windows, sundial at corner and pantiled courtyard buildings.

South Kersie, 18th/19th century, T-plan farmhouse, humbler than Kersie Mains but solid and characterful, piended roof, whitewashed with painted margins and quoins. **South Doll**, small single-storey steading with heptagonal horse-mill. **Westfield**, one-and-a-half storey, with three dormers, sits sedately within trim walled garden area staring out over the Carselands; farmyard tucked away behind.

Club's Tomb, Linkfield, 18th century
Ruin of small stone mausoleum, said to have been built by James Club of Airth, who wished to be buried in it, with his dog, to escape resurrectionists! Barrel-vaulted within, tomb now sports grassy top-knot with sprouting saplings.

Dunmore Pottery, 1860s (demolished 1967)
Piended double block of kiln-workers' cottages and manager's house, in white render with black surrounds, all that remains of this famous pottery.

Above *Peter Gardner's kiln, Dunmore Pottery*. Right *Torwood Castle*.

In the 1860s, Peter Gardner, whose interests included breeding and training Arab steeds, transformed an existing local pottery into one with a national reputation, expanding its repertoire from the local red clay ware to include the famous blue, green and crimson glazes that became his trademark.

34 **Torwood Castle**, from 14th century
Part ruined three- and four-storey L-plan tower house, 1566, with courtyard, for Sir Alexander Forrester of the Forresters of Garden and Torwood, situated high up in what was once a royal forest. Peppered with gun loops, square

stairtower in angle contains castle's entrance, above which, moulded frame has decorative panel with shell motif. Restoration from 1950s, Gordon Millar, taken on by Torwood Castle Trust, future uncertain. Remains of **courtyard** and **well**.

Broch, The Tappoch, Tor Wood,
possibly Early Iron Age
On brink of rocky slope, vestige of tapered stone tower, 80ft in diameter, 20ft high, with walls some 15ft thick at the base constructed from large rough blocks from neighbouring cliffs and outcrops. Stair recess in walls and narrow entrance through banking. Amazing survival and best preserved of the Lowland brochs, first excavated in 1864. One of 10 such structures in the Tay, Forth and Tweed districts, their purpose remains conjectural, but most likely to be defensive dwellings erected by wandering colonists.

Finds include three boulders with cup-and-ring markings, saddle and rotary querns, whorls and other small stone objects, hand-made coarse pottery shards, some preserved Museum of Antiquities, Royal Museum of Scotland and Callender House Museum.

DENNY AND DUNIPACE
Separated by the River Carron, the word *Denny* is considered by some to be a corruption of *dun* the Gaelic for hill, Dunipace was thought to transalate as 'Hill of Peace'. Both settlements owed their relative importance to their strategic position at an important road and river crossing. Castles on the banks of the Carron such as Graham, Rankine, Herbertshire and Torwood

In the late Middle Ages, the Tor Wood was an area of the Royal Forest, and the office of Forester was held, from the second half of the 15th century until the middle 17th century by the Forestars of Garden. Sir Alexander Forestar of Garden (d.1598) was for a time Provost of Stirling. Early in the 17th century, the estate of Garden passed to the Stirling family, but the Forestars retained their office of Royal Foresters until the 1600s when the Tor Wood was acquired by George, First Lord Forrester of Corstorphine. The buildings at Torwood Castle enclosing the courtyard are probably the work of the new owner.

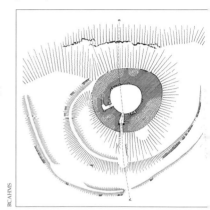

Top *Broch, Tor Wood.* Middle *Blairs Farm.* Above *Carbrook (demolished), once part of Torwood Estates.*

Following the decline of the wool and calico industries in the early 19th century, Denny switched to paper-making with huge success. Eleven mills, including Herbertshire, Carrongrove and Stoneywood, situated along a 1½ mile stretch of the Carron, were eventually to make Denny the centre of paper making in Scotland in the 1950s.

DUNIPACE

DENNY

71

DENNY AND DUNIPACE

*In the division called Temple Denny, and within a mile of the new bridge over Carron, on the road to Fintry, about five miles west from Denny, there is a cascade called **Auchenlillylin-spout**. In the first year of the present century, the wild natural beauties of the spot were transformed into a sort of fairyland, by the genius of Robert Hill WS, Edinburgh, who had purchased the lands of Forrest Hill, of which it is a part. A rustic cottage of whinstone, with the rustic points facing one in all directions, was built on the very margin of a deep fissure, through which the waters of Carron flow, to be tossed over the rock of Auchenlilly, within perhaps six yards of the heath-covered cottage.*
By the Revd John Dempster for *The New Statistical Account*, 1845

supplied both leaders and soldiers to the armies of Robert Bruce and William Wallace.

In 18th and 19th centuries, the soft and pure waters of the Carron brought industry to the area, from paper making to calico printing, later supplemented by iron founding and coal mining. Current development initiatives link Denny and Dunipace with neighbouring Bonnybridge.

Temple Denny Road commemorates the time during 12th and 13th centuries when the district of **Dryburgh**, surrounding the central dun, was owned by the Order of the Knights Templar. Later a centre for paper, flax, iron goods and coal.

35 **The Braes**, late 18th century
Handsome farmhouse, on hillside north west of Dunipace, in white harl with black trim to windows, doors, wall and even chimney quoins, commanding spectacular views over Carron valley from balustraded terrace. Doric porch, with marriage lintel dated 1643 with initials *JF* (James Forrester) and *AC* (Agnes Crawford), presumably from earlier property on the site.

Braes Fort, Iron Age
Petrified trace of small rectangular fort within ruinous stone wall, on rocky knoll near farmhouse, some 150ft by 85ft, with walls 10ft thick.

Top *The Braes*. Above *Doorway detail, The Braes*. Right *Quarter House*.

The Knights Templar were a society of monastic knights, dedicated to defending the Holy Sepulchre and pilgrims to Jerusalem, founded in 1118 and dissolved in 1312 by the Pope. Existing in all Christian lands, one of their greatest and richest centres was London, where their activities were greatly encouraged by the crusading zeal of Richard I, *Coeur de Lion*. The Templars' ancient church still stands near the Strand. In Denny, the knights owned the district of Dryburgh surrounding the central dun. It is not known whether this name was acquired by its association with the great abbey of that name.

36 **Quarter House**, 1776
Small Georgian house of considerable quality, remodelled early 19th century, two storey, white harled, dressed margins and quoins. Beneath slated pavilion roof, central mini-pediment with bullseye window and double Tuscan-columned entrance porch; courtyard additions to rear. Until 1630, lands of Quarter were owned by the Livingston family (see p.32-3).

DENNY

Denny Cross, Broad Street

Hub of the town, Broad Street contains some original vernacular houses. **No 1**, late 18th century, having rolled skewputts, **Nos 3 & 5**, with pilastered ground-floor façade, dated 1812 on tablet above moulded eaves course. Bay-windowed **Criterion Bar**, 1890, and white-and-black liveried **Railway Hotel** command the corners. Central cast-iron **drinking fountain** removed 1939. In 1890s, two thatched cottages, one with forestair, formed part of the north side of Broad Street.

37 **Parish Church**, rebuilt 1813

Rubble with three-stage square bell tower, 1838, short slated spire and weathervane providing dramatic stop to Broad Street. Chancel added 1928. Thomas Johnstone of Hallhouse buried in graveyard (see p.78).

Top *Broad Street c.1890, looking towards the Parish Church and Denny Cross.*
Above *3 & 5 Broad Street.*

38 **Shopping Centre**, Church Walk, 1960s, Wilson & Wilson

Extensive U-shaped shopping complex, canopied shopping below, flats and maisonettes over; two-storey octagonal unit at end acting as the knuckle to Duke Street. In pink and ochre stripes like an ice-cream sundae, inappropriate contextually but with a certain brash charm.

Below *Parish Church.* Middle *Shopping Centre.* Bottom *St Patrick's Primary School.*

Stirling Street

East side has good early 19th-century vernacular buildings, some stone, some colour-washed with contrasting surrounds.

St Alexander's RC Church, 1889

Split-level, Romanesque gable to road, crypt at lower level. **Denny Workspace** (former St Patrick's RC Primary School), Carrongrove Crescent, 1932, A N Malcolm, Stirling County Council Architects, in orange harl and slated, ingenious radiating plan about octagonal hub. **St Patrick's Primary School**, 1981, Central Regional Council Architectural Services, single storey in dark brick with linked pavilions overlooking playing fields.

Above *Registrar's Office*. Right *Herbertshire Street Housing*.

Registrar's Office, No 107, 1910
Wide-awake two-storey former Denny Parish Council Offices, with gables topped by Masonic finials, crest of the town above ground-floor window, Gibbs doorway to underline civic role.

Herbertshire Street Housing, 1975, Wheeler & Sproson
Parallel two-storey terraces, for Scottish Special Housing Association, step down hill towards squat flatted blocks at Gill Street; private and public spaces sensitively defined by low fencing and stone walls.

Below from top *Town House; Denny Day Nursery; 53-59 Glasgow Road; Visual Information Systems*.

39 **Glasgow Road**
Single and semidetached Victorian villas line this main route south, modern housing to west, football ground, old foundry site and fields to east. **Town House**, 1931, James Strang & Wilson, anachronistic Scots Baronial, in grey rubble with dressed margins, crowsteps and arched entrance under battlemented three-storey tower. Costing £12,500, it was described by the *Stirling Observer* as: *quaintly interesting in design rather than imposing*. **Denny Day Nursery**, 1981, Central Regional Council Architectural Services, pleasantly scaled single storey in buff brick with mansard roof over projecting bays; imaginative playground with traffic lights and railway signals. **Nos 53-59**, 1890s, four-in-a-row presents neatly balanced composition of end gables, bays and dormers. **Rupheim**, bay-windowed cottage with dormers and handsome oversailing roof.

40 **Visual Information Systems**, 1937
Crisp single-storey classical frontage of former offices of Cruickshanks and Co., Denny Iron Works, in brick and stone, pavilion roof behind balustrading, triple windows flank central pediment with Doric columns and pilasters.

41 **Denny High School**, 1959, Alison & Hutchison & Partners
Extensive flat-roofed cruciform school, on hill known as Glororum and previously a popular

golf course, with distinctive five-storey glazed tower, frame picked out in bright yellow.

Bingo and Social Club, 1939
Former Cinema de Luxe presents wild-west façade to Glasgow Road, site of original Town Hall, destroyed by fire, 1937.

Denny High School.

Duke Street
Broompark Centre, remodelled 1881, J J Burnet
Much-mutilated rubble former Broompark Church with arched windows at gallery level; porch, remains of chancel and small single-storey hall.

Clydesdale Bank, 1866
Pleasantly surprising, white-harled, two-storey gothic villa, windows and doorway enlivened with quixotic assortment of curved and angular hoodmouldings.

Westpark Church, 1900, James Strang
Gothic exercise in brown rubble with octagonal tower and slated spire. Unfortunate flat-roofed concrete block extension, 1979.

Above Clydesdale Bank. Left 30 Duke Street.

30 Duke Street, 1880s, (?)James Strang
Exemplary villa, behind shielding evergreens, distinguished by ornate consoled pediments over blind arching to first-floor windows and generously angled bays trimmed with filigree ironwork.

Denny Public School, 1890s, A McC Mitchell (demolished 1990s)
Strictly classical and well proportioned in creamy brown stone, advanced centre bay capped by rhythmical balustrading between mini-pediments. A building of some distinction that should have been kept! It linked, in interesting

There are no begging poor, belonging to the Parish, but there are a number of housekeepers in indigent circumstances, who receive occasional supplies from the collections, made at the church doors, on Sunday. The men are almost all engaged in husbandry, and the women generally in spinning. A number of boys and girls are employed at a print-field, and a cotton manufactory, in the neighbouring parish of Dunipace.
From Revd Thomas Fergus' report for Sir John Sinclair's Statistical Account of Scotland, 1791

stylistic contrast, to single-storey gothic T-plan **Denny Primary School**, with cosily proportioned moonrocket spire in north-east angle.

DUNIPACE

Dunipace Old Church, 1834, William Stirling Gaunt gothic ashlar, isolated on a wooded bluff overlooking the Carron valley, with square bell tower, topped by ornately pierced crenellations, replacing former 16th-century church. Dunipace and Larbert, were formely chapels belonging to the Abbey of Cambuskenneth. Proposed conversion to housing, 2001.

Top Denny Public School. Above Dunipace Old Church. Right Denovan House.

Cambuskenneth Abbey, 13th century Founded c.1147 by David I, to the east of Stirling within a loop of the River Forth, and of which only the bell tower survives today, was a daughter house of the French Augustinian monastery of St Nicholas of Arras. Dunipace and Larbert were only two of the abbey's many endowments within the district. The canons of the abbey were also granted fishing rights in the Forth and payments from the rents of the crown lands about Stirling. At the Reformation, the lands of Cambuskenneth were elected into a temporal lordship and eventually came into the hands of the Earl of Mar. *Stirlingshire*, RCAHMS. See also *Stirling and the Trossachs* in this series.

42 **Denovan House**, from mid-18th century Substantial Jacobethan ashlar mansion, 1843–5 recasting of Georgian villa, with decorated pediment, ornamental strapwork and balustrading to bay window and porch. Gleaming white, late 19th-century conservatory adjoins. Elaborate Jacobethan interiors in dining and billiard rooms; drawing room with moulded architraves, marble chimneypiece and original pendant lights. Once the property of the Johnstones of Alva, who made money in India; purchased in 1830s by William Forbes of Callendar House (see p.33) James Graham Adam acquired portion of estate with bleachfield and altered and extended the house in 1843–5.

Within grounds, mid-19th-century **stables**, now altered; square **gatepiers**, 1843–5, with rounded corniced caps. House at centre of radiating formal avenues to each point on the

Below Denovan Mains. Right Unexecuted scheme for Denovan House by Robert Adam.

compass, and diagonally, like saltire cross, with bleachfield to the east.

Denovan Mains, from 17th century
Picturesque whitewashed courtyard farm with curved stairtower to rear.

Dunipace House, 1792 (demolished late 1940s)
Classical, five bays, pilastered and grandly pedimented under hipped roof, at one time the grandest mansion in the area, built by the Spottiswoodes to replace original House of Dunipace (associated with the Livingstons who held the property from late 15th to mid-17th century). Library addition, 1890s, Hippolyte Blanc. Restored after a fire in 1897 and at one time in the possession of Forbes of Callendar.

Dunipace Park
Secluded among evergreens, ruined octagonal **stairtower**, converted to doocot, all that remains of original House of Dunipace. **Watch-house**, vaulted **mausoleum** and 17th-century gravestones in adjacent atmospheric graveyard.

Hills of Dunipace
Curious conical wooded mounds, reputed to be man-made peace offerings to the gods, Dunipace meaning 'Hill of Peace' and named after allegedly strenuous battle between Picts and Scots at Skaithmuir. Truth probably more mundane, such natural outcroppings being in all likelihood glacial drumlins. Near here was found the famous **Dunipace Brooch**.

43 **Herbertshire Castle**, from 13th century
Lofty L-plan dominated by four-storey rectangular and battlemented tower, destroyed by fire in 1914. Legendary birthplace of the Black Douglas, owned latterly by Lady Forbes of Callendar. Grounds now public park.

Tygetshaugh Court, 1987,
Falkirk District Council Architects
Neatly scaled flats and cottages for the elderly in buff brick and slates with projecting bays in dark stained wood; common room with pyramid roof.

McCabes, early 19th century
Traditional Denny howff painted dark green with white trim. Beneath decorative pediment, marriage inscription and date, 1722. Sundial on gable tabling.

Dunipace House.

The estate of Dunipace is in the parish of the same name. It is a beautiful place, and worthy of the many romantic and historic associations which cluster about it. The ancient mansion house of Dunipace is supposed to have been similar in design to Torwood mansion, the ruins of which are still to be seen. From J C Gibson, Lands and Lairds of Larbert & Dunipace Parishes

Best known of the antiquarian finds in the district is the Dunipace Brooch, 700–800 AD. Silver-gilt brooch with hinged circular head inset with amber and decorated front and back with interlacing animal patterns of a type more commonly found in Ireland. One of only two found in Scotland.

Below *Hill of Dunipace.*
Bottom *Tygetshaugh Court.*

Top *Dunipace Free Church.*
Above *Carrongrove House.*

Thomas Johnstone of Hallhouse, 1799–1885, farmer and shoemaker, was one of a long line of his family to farm Holehouse as it was known in those days. His diary is one of those rare documents whose very existence warms the cockles of the heart. Written on re-used paper and bound with cobbler's twine, it records for over 40 years not only his day-to-day activities but his views on wider affairs obtained from newspapers and books of which he was an avid reader. On one occasion at least he pawned his watch to buy some books he wanted. A single entry, that of 12 September 1846, will give a flavour: *Read the papers – sheared grass and went to Hays to get stackhead straw – saw his new wife (appearit carefull and discreet) – day excessive warm and dry – cholera carries off 900 men of 2 regiments and half of the inhabitants of Kurachee – since the 19th August there has been the finest weather – only 2 showers – most seasonable – corn now mostly in.*
John Reid, 'The Diary of Thomas Johnstone of Hallhouse', *Calatria No 1*

Right *Strathcarron Hospice.*
Below *Hallhouse.*

44 Dunipace Free Church, 1890, W Simpson
Robust gothic church with tapered tower, on prominent corner site, short spire springing from behind parapet balcony with corner bartizans and gargoyles; church itself strongly buttressed, with large five-light window in gable. Yawning entrance porch in angle.

WEST DENNY
West Denny and particularly Carronglen formerly held much of the local industry, the dozen or so mills clustering in the valley to take advantage of the soft waters of the Carron, some of which remain. Today, pleasant walks by the river and the views as the road climbs steeply towards Fankerton and the Fintry hills attract the visitor.

45 Stoneywood Park, 1950s
Semidetached millworkers' houses, variously colour-washed with ornamental doorpieces. Denny was the centre of paper making in Scotland during 1950s, **Stoneywood Mill** specialising in manila papers made from rope, rags and wood pulp.

Carrongrove House, (?)Andrew Heiton, *c.*1855–75
In stone, distinguished by decorative oriel over slim entrance porch, head office of Carrongrove Paper Mill, down in the valley. Demolished **lodge** had decorative slating and fine filigree ironwork to ridge and finials (see colour p.86).

Strathcarron Hospice
Large mill-owner's villa, formerly Randolph Hill, with handsome Voyseyian projecting porch; large **extension**, 1997–8, Alistair Keyte, with sweeping roof, mature trees and finely landscaped grounds.

Fankerton
Early 19th-century millworkers' houses, at top of hill, built for Carrongrove Paper Company.

45A Hallhouse (or Holehouse), from late 16th century
Elongated, harled, crowstepped and slated farm,

situated on ridge among trees, radically remodelled 1990s, to a square box. Marriage lintels indicate this has been the home of the Johnstone family since the 16th century.

45B **Hall**, early 1800s
Dignified dormered cottage in white render with painted window surrounds and edge trim, at end of leafy driveway; undoubtedly the home of a bonnet laird in former times.

Castle Rankine
No visible traces remain of 13th-century castle of Sir Herbert de Morham, but archaeological excavations indicate a tower with barbican some 100ft square. Interesting and enjoyable walks follow the Castle Rankine and Little Denny burns with their two reservoirs, **Drumbowie** and **Little Denny**.

Top *Hall*. Middle *High Street, view towards Cowden Hill.*

BONNYBRIDGE
Growing at a strategic crossing of the Bonny Water, squeezed beside the Forth & Clyde Canal, Bonnybridge owed its development in modern times to the manufacture of cooking and heating appliances and firebricks. The course of the Antonine Wall, crossing between the Forth & Clyde Canal and the railway, is to be seen at its best here especially at Seabegs Wood and at the wall fort of Rough Castle.

46 **Bonnybridge Parish Church**, 1877, Alexander Watt
In grey Thornleydike stone, broad-shouldered neo-gothic church with side aisles and belfry, steeply pedimented entrance porch under handsome four-lancet window with quatrefoil tracery. Built with substantial contributions from Smith & Wellstood Ironfounders.

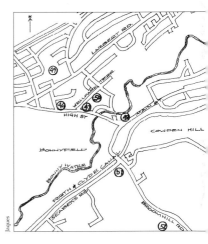

Bonnybridge Parish Church.

Location on the **Forth & Clyde Canal** was more important to Bonnybridge than to Falkirk, which had other options for transportation of their goods. Between 1854 and 1877, several ironworks were founded in the area including Columbian Stove Works, 1860, Bonnybridge Foundry, 1870 and Broomhill Foundry, 1877.

47 Royal Hotel, High Street, *c.*1900

Three storeys in familiar white-and-black decor, its curved corner, pedimented top-floor windows and wallhead chimney dominate this part of town. Essential Bonnybridge landmark for over 200 years, much altered.

Smithfield, mid-19th century

Quoined windows, wallhead chimney and bargeboarded dormers, formerly an alehouse favoured by canal boatmen; one of the town's oldest buildings.

48 War Memorial Park, 1960s

Splendid rococo ironwork arch and pillars, at busy junction, give access to peaceful setting round obelisk memorial to the two World Wars.

49 Wheatlands, Larbert Road

Six-bay mansion with flanking wings in grey ashlar, pavilion roof at one time with filigree iron ridge decoration and Doric doorpiece. On raised terrace overlooking sloping gardens; until 1952 home of the Ure family, directors of Smith & Wellstood. Much remodelled, now retirement home.

Bonnybridge Health Centre, 1989, Common Services Agency

Trim single-storey quadrangular block, on part of former Wheatlands estate, in brown facing brick and roughcast with shallow pitched roof over.

Hopepark Terrace

Very pleasant group of sheltered houses, single-storey four-in-a-block cottages with small loggias, set among trees.

From top Royal Hotel; War Memorial Park; Wheatlands; Bonnybridge Health Centre; Hopepark Terrace. *Right* Bonnybridge Hospital.

Bonnybridge Hospital, Falkirk Road, 1987, Common Services Agency

In brown brick with shallow pitched roof, long, low block with projecting wings, sitting out area with pergola to west.

Top *Falkirk 1824, with Tattie Kirk to right, Parish Church and Steeple at centre and the billowing smoke of Carron Iron Company to left.* Above *Falkirk town centre.* Right *Stained glass from South Bantaskine House in the Howgate Shopping Centre.* Below *Postcard view of Newmarket Street, Falkirk c.1900.*

Above *King's Court, Falkirk.* Callendar House: Right *Cromwell stair and painted ceiling;* Middle *Hamilton Library;* Below *South front.* Bottom *Graeme High School, Falkirk.* Bottom right *Bantaskine Boat House, Falkirk.*

Jaques

Falkirk Museums

A I L S T Tourist Board

Falkirk Museums

Keith Hunter

Jaques

Top left *Watling Lodge, Tamfourhill.* Top *Rosebank by Richard Jaques.* Left *The Falkirk Wheel and Visitor Centre under construction.* Above *Falkirk Wheel skims the rooftops of Carmuirs.* Below *CAD image of the Falkirk Wheel and Visitor Centre when complete.*

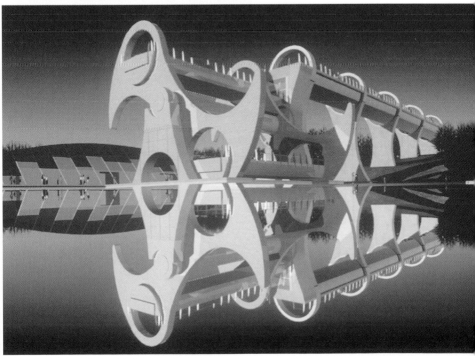

Top *St Mary's of the Angels RC Church, Falkirk.*
Top right *Accommodation for the Elderly,
Bellsdyke Hospital, North Larbert.* Above
*Gateway of former Grahamston Ironworks,
Falkirk.* Right *James Bruce of Kinnaird by
Pompeo Batoni.* Below *Dunmore Park.*

Jaques

Jaques

Jaques

Jaques

A I L L S T Tourist Board

Top and middle left *The Pineapple, Dunmore.* Middle *The riverbank Dunmore Model Village.* Above *The Carse looking toward Kincardine power station.* Left *Dunmore Model Village.*

85

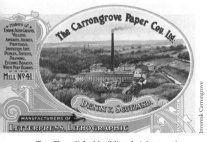

Top *Demolished building-height mural depicting Smith & Wellstood's Columbian Stoveworks, Bonnybridge.* Middle *Antonine Wall at Seabegs Wood, Bonnybridge.* Above *Carrongrove Paper Company advert from 1905.* Right *Stained glass on the stairway of Carrongrove House.*

Paul Kirkwood

BP plc (2001)

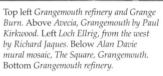

Top left *Grangemouth refinery and Grange Burn.* Above *Avecia, Grangemouth by Paul Kirkwood.* Left *Loch Ellrig, from the west by Richard Jaques.* Below *Alan Davie mural mosaic, The Square, Grangemouth.* Bottom *Grangemouth refinery.*

Jaques

Jaques

Scotsman Publications Ltd

Right *Church of the Holy Rood,*
Grangemouth. Below *The Arbour Room,*
Kinneil House. Below right *View from*
Stewart Avenue, Bo'ness across the town
to the River Forth and beyond to Fife.
Middle *Staff house, Hope Cottages,*
Muirhouses. Bottom left *Sculpted stones,*
east foreshore, Bo'ness. Bottom right
Postcard view from Upper Bo'ness to
Lower, c.1909.

Crown Copyright: reproduced courtesy of Historic Scotland

Jaques

50 Wellpark

Site of very pleasant undulating park formed from cutting for the old Bonnybridge and Kilsyth railway line. **Wellpark Terrace**, 1890, plain but well-crafted two-storey stone terracing built for workers of Smith & Wellstood.

Seabegs Road
Caledonia House, 1890s

Industrial red brick baroque with stone quoins, keystones and embellishments, square porch with round-headed pediment (demolition due 2001). **Bonnybridge Direct Works**, 1984, Central Regional Council Architectural Services, neat little office block in buff brick with deep slated and mansarded fascia.

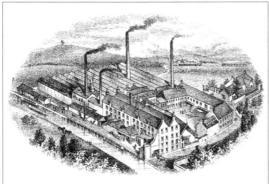

Top *Wellpark.* Middle *Wellpark Terrace.* Above *Royal Bank of Scotland, Bridge Street.*

Left *Smith & Wellstood Columbian Stove Works.* Below *Smith & Wellstood Offices.*

51 Smith & Wellstood Offices, 1930s

Flat-roofed, in roughcast with brick panels, south of the canal, articulated block at corner with flagpoles and shell-canopied drinking fountain for the thirsty worker. Behind were the foundry buildings, demolished late 1990s, replaced by housing. Columbian Stove Works opened, 1860, modernised foundry opened, 1951 (see colour p.86).

52 Antonine Primary School, Broomhill Road, 1988,

Central Regional Council Architectural Services Smart single-storey in white roughcast with deep red painted fascia, slated pavilion and gable roof.

Smith and Wellstood, Bonnybridge, 1860 James Smith learned to work with iron in America. On returning to Scotland in 1854 he designed and assembled stoves but contracted out the castings until he and his partner, Stephen Wellstood, a tinsmith to trade, opened the works in which tin, copper and bronze were used.

Bonnyside House, early 19th century

Large white-rendered L-plan villa, secluded among trees by reservoir, with pedimented porch in the angle.

Best-surviving part of the rampart and ditch of the Antonine Wall is from Tentfield Plantation to Bonnyside House, almost 1½ miles including the fort at Rough Castle.

Bonnyside House.

In 1300 King Robert the Bruce was nearly killed by a wild white bull while he was out hunting in Seabegs. These animals had their stamping grounds in the woods of Stirlingshire, roaming the woods of Castlecary, which was part of the Barony of Seabegs. The Bruce may have been a guest at the castle whose owner, Straiton of Straiton, fought on his side at the Battle of Bannockburn in 1314.

Seabegs Motte, 12th century
Ancient defensive artificial mound (which would have had wooden tower), north of the Antonine Wall; referred to in a 1542 charter as: *lie Mot de Seybeggis*.

Antonine Wall, Seabegs Wood
Only 450m long, this well-preserved stretch of the Roman wall, ditch and outer mound is the best-surviving section of the Military Way. Although there are no visible signs of a fort between Rough Castle and Castlecary, distance between the two suggests intermediate station at east end of Seabegs Wood (see colour p.86).
Historic Scotland; open to the public

Above *Lilia, Rough Castle*. Right *Rough Castle*.

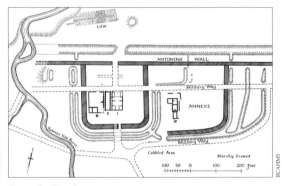

From 1770s–85, when the Falkirk Trysts were held at Rough Castle, their second site after their move from Reddingmuir to the east, Bonnybridge and the roads in the Valley of the Bonny saw thousands of cattle pass over them. **Drove Loan** today commemorates those days as does **Tentfield Wood** where the tents were set up for those attending the trysts.

53 **Rough Castle**
Square plan, measuring only 215ft each way within the rampart giving internal area of just over one acre, second-smallest but best-preserved fort on the Antonine Wall. Protected by the Rowan Tree Burn, the Carron Valley and shallow trough of marshy ground to the south, only easy access was from the east. Inside, remains of three stone buildings: headquarters erected by the Cohort of Nervii commemorated on inscribed tablet found within, granary with loading platform and commandant's house, large, rectangular consisting of series of rooms ranged round open courtyard. Post-holes of timber-framed buildings, presumably barracks, also found. Relics from the site now in the Museum of Antiquities, Royal Museum of Scotland, Edinburgh, include three fragments of a building inscription and an altar.
Annexe outside the defences, slightly larger than the fort, included bathhouse. Beyond the ditch, infamous *lilia*, or lilies, series of concealed defensive pits with pointed stakes for the unwary, some still visible, arranged in 10 parallel rows.

St Joseph's RC Church, Broomhill Road, 1925
Italianate aisled church and priest's house, in brick
and cream render, with louvred bell tower, on hill
with appropriate evergreens bringing a touch of
Tuscany to northern parts. In front, impressive
perron stair flanking small shrine; church hall
below. **St Joseph's Primary School**, 1989, Central
Regional Council Architectural Services, ingenious
single-storey lozenge-shaped plan around central
top-lit hall; in white roughcast with slated roof.

St Helen's Church, Church Street, 1934, B Wilson
Powerful exercise in Scottish Romanesque;
rectangular plan in rubble over ashlar base,
arched entrance porch in projecting crowstepped
tower, up high by the railway line with
spectacular views to north and south.

HIGH BONNYBRIDGE
From St Helen's it is worthwhile taking the road
south under the railway bridge to explore the
undulating scenery by way of High Bonnybridge
and Drum Wood.

GREENHILL
Greenhill School, 1890, James Strang
(demolished 1990s)
In stone, with hints of Mackintosh in the detailing
of doors and bay windows.

DENNYLOANHEAD
Now somewhat cut off from its near namesake to
the north by the M876 east/west motorway,
Dennyloanhead is the starting point for some of
the best walks in Falkirk district. Across the
canal, there is Castlecary to the west, Garbethill
to the south and the extensive woods above High
Bonnybridge to the south east.

Head of Muir Primary School, 1978
Central Regional Council Architectural Services
In brown facing brick with deep-slated fascias,
ingenious irregular zig-zag plan of linked
pavilions, each with central rooflight in swept
pavilion roof.

Top St Joseph's Primary School.
Above St Helen's Church.

Stein of Bonnybridge, 1888
At the end of the 19th century, firebricks
became an increasingly important item
both in the domestic market and for the
iron industry. Competing with such
giants as The Glenboig Brick Company,
at that time the largest in Britain, Steins
of Bonnybridge with their works at
Milnquarter, Denny and Castlecary
very soon established themselves as a
worthy competitor.

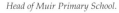

Head of Muir Primary School.

Dennyloanhead Church

Jaques

Dennyloanhead Church, 1738
Tall white harled box with three slim lancets,
much more interesting inside than out, the
interior serene and friendly, pale blue
Adamesque ceiling floating over all, corbelled
heads at beam ends. Enlarged, galleries and
lancet lights added 1815, belfry, 1930s. Now a
fireplace showroom. Adjoining stone **Muirhead
Memorial Hall**, 1893, gifted to church, 1930s.
Georgian stone **manse**, 1850s, with decorative
quoins and Doric doorpiece under pavilion roof.

Crown Hotel, 18th century
White painted ashlar and black window
surrounds, traditional hotel garb, commanding
prominent position at junction of Glasgow and
Bonnybridge Roads.

Jaques

HAGGS
Haggs Church, 1840, David Rhind
Small, very elegant, finely detailed in warm brown
stone; large porch extension at front with triple
round-headed windows over wide arched
entrance. Octagonal belfry to main gable. (See
similar church by Rhind at Camelon, p.45.)

Margaret Avenue, 1930s
Interestingly modelled flat-roofed blocks with
corner windows exploiting panoramic views and
projecting concrete eyebrows.

Jaques

Castlecary Mill Farm, mid-19th century
Plain gabled farmhouse and yard in storybook
setting with bridge and trees; old mill wheel at
gable of steading.

54 **Castle Cary**, from 1480 (*below*)
Four-storey tower house with crowstepped

Jaques

Jaques

RCAHMS

caphouse, for the Livingstons, cadet branch of the Earls of Callendar, in beautiful secluded and wooded position on south bank of the Castle Glen. Lower extension to east, 1679, when castle passed to the Balliols, descended, it is said, from King John Balliol. Pistol loup near front door a reminder that defensive measures were still necessary at that relatively late date.

Red Burn Viaduct, Castlecary, 1842, John Miller Majestic eight spans of dressed stone, for the Edinburgh and Glasgow Railway, with segmental arches, now strengthened with old rails.

BANKNOCK
Bankier School, 1965, Stirling County Council Architects
Dark brown brick, flat-roofed school, amid trees of the old estate, with dark-stained timber fascias and bright blue panel inserts. Now much altered.

Gordon Arms, 1890s
Lumpy white L-plan villa, heavily quoined, pedimented Doric porch in the angle. **Banknock Home Farm**, 18th century, derelict, pleasantly scaled single-storey with arched entrance under central pediment. **Lodge House**, a little gem, in ashlar with exquisitely detailed rectangular bay, the whole happily cherished by owners. Banknock House, long since gone.

Bankier Distillery, 1828 (demolished)
Founded by Daniel McFarlane and incorporating two pyramid-roofed kilns, it was connected to Forth & Clyde Canal by horse tramway, wharf remaining.

ALLANDALE
In Dumfries stone, two fine long rows of single-storey **cottages**, 1919–22, flank main road. Built to provide accommodation for Castlecary workforce of Stein of Bonnybridge, firebrick manufacturers. All had inside baths and lavatories, not always the case in houses of that period.

Opposite from top Dennyloanhead Church; Manse; Crown Hotel; Haggs Church; Margaret Avenue; Caringrew Farm; Castle Cary.

Roman Fort, Castlecary
Oblong on plan with an enclosed area of 3½ acres, the main defence consisted of a stone wall round all four sides. On a rounded knoll protected by the valley of the Bonny Water, it has been raided for building materials regularly and seriously damaged in 1841 when the Edinburgh/Glasgow Railway was built diagonally across it, the modern road causing further damage. Within, on south-west corner, 15ft square tower probably matched by similar at south east, headquarters building, granary, internal bathhouse, discovered 1796 and planned by General Roy, latrine, rubbish-pit and part of the internal drainage system. Also fortified five-sided annexe east of fort covering 2½ acres.
RCAHMS, *Stirlingshire*

On Friday 10 December, 1937, the Edinburgh/Glasgow express collided with the preceding Dundee/Glasgow train just beyond Castlecary Station killing 35 passengers.
'The Castlecary Railway Disaster', John Walker, *Calatria No 11*

Top *Red Burn Viaduct*. Middle *Lodge House*. Above *Bankier Distillery*. Left *Allandale*.

Top *Underwood Lockhouse*. Right *Polmont c.1920*. Middle *Polmont Old Parish Church*. Above *Memorial, churchyard.*

The Hart Children Tombstone, Polmont Old Parish churchyard
Under simple carving of three castles in a shield, the emblems of a mason, with two flanking figures the inscription reads:
HERE lyes Christian Hart daughter to Robert Hart Mason in Reading she died May 8 1745 aged 2 years. Also Mary Heart died October 19th 1752, aged 3 years ... months. Also Janet Heart died Sept 2 1760 aged 2 years 2 months. Also Helen Hart died July 26th 1766 aged 11 years.

Underwood Lockhouse, early 19th century Hostelry formed from row of two-storey lock-keepers' cottages and stables; car park on line of Antonine Wall.

POLMONT
Lying south east of Falkirk, Polmont was part of the great landholdings of Abbotskerse belonging to Holyrood Abbey until the Reformation when, with the splitting up of the monastic estates, it fell into the hands of the Earls, later Dukes, of Hamilton, the present duke enjoying the subsidiary title of Lord Polmont.

Polmont's mineral wealth was such that it was soon able to separate from Falkirk, becoming its own parish in 1724. Continuing commercial success brought many fine mansions, Millfield, one-time home of the Stein family, Polmont Park, Polmont House, Parkhill, home of the Gray-Buchanans, and for their sons, Blair Lodge School at Brightons, one of the first public schools modelled on English lines.

Today Polmont's northern boundary is defined by the motorway, its southern by canal and railway, while the wriggling Polmont Burn to the south west performs a complete about-turn as it joins the Westquarter Burn on its journey to the Carselands and the mouth of the river at Grangemouth.

Bo'ness Road
Polmont Old Parish Church, 1844, John Tait
Grey ashlar, Italian Romanesque entered through handsome arched doorway with hoodmoulding terminating in bearded heads in pedimented porch (see p.3). Sadly, now physically separated from its parish by the motorway, its two proud three-stage towers are nevertheless a familiar sight to travellers. Original **Parish Church**, 1731, picturesque roofless and ivy-clad ruin. Within,

family tomb of the Gray-Buchanans. Churchyard includes **memorial stones** to the victims of the 1923 Redding Pit Disaster (see p.99).

Kenneil House, 1735
Plain yet handsome, three-bay, two-storey former manse, harled with quoins, window margins and rusticated entrance architrave. Bay-windowed Victorian extension to west.

Main Street
Lacking cohesion despite many above-average housing developments on either side, such as Avonlea and Millfield. Characterful **Black Bull**, white harled with black door and window surrounds, deserves better company. **Community Centre**, *c*.1900, compact L-plan, stone and slated former Polmont Female School, with two porches and bell tower in the angle. **Rosehall**, two-storey harled Georgian villa, with both margined and hoodmoulded windows and plain stone porch.

Turret Hall, *c*.1840
Splendid battlemented and buttressed gothic folly with two-storey finialed entrance bay clamped between circular turrets.

Avonlea Drive, 1964, Philip Cocker & Partners
North of Main Street, sensitive layout of linked single- and two-storey houses for Link Housing Association, with tiled monopitch roofs, and four-storey flat-roofed flatted block, all in white harl, in fine landscaping of former Polmont Park House estate.

Polmont Park House, 1750s (demolished)
Courtyard **stable block** all that remains of '*genteel house*', advertised for sale in 1793, added to twice in 19th century and demolished, 1960s. Grounds now entered through modern housing layout.

Weedingshall Youth Care Centre, 1989, Central Regional Council Architectural Services
Irregular buff brick development, in sloping grounds of Weedingshall House, with red tiled roof and projecting bays, decorative quoins to window surrounds. Now closed.

Oakbank Sheltered Housing, 1980, Central Regional Council Architectural Services
Pleasantly relaxed group in buff brick, with red tile monopitch roof and sitting-out areas, tucked into the banking.

From top Kenneil House; Main Street and Black Bull; Community Centre; Turret Hall; Avonlea Drive; Weedingshall Youth Care Centre.

Top *Entrance front, Parkhill House.* Right *Rear elevation, Parkhill House.* Above *Millfield, c.1909, built for John Miller, civil engineer of the Edinburgh and Glasgow Railway.*

The Gray-Buchanan family of Parkhill was very active in all kinds of local charitable works especially those associated with education, healthcare and child welfare.

Below *Polmont House.*
Bottom *St Margaret's Primary School.*

Polmont Bank Lodge, late 18th century
Another survivor, in ashlar, integrated into estate wall, bracketed pavilion roof.

55 **Parkhill House**, 1789, James Cheape
Three-storey home of the Gray-Buchanans, excellent example of classical taste in small country house, with partly sunk basement, hipped and slated roof above moulded eaves course, set in magnificent grounds (now Gray-Buchanan Park). Original entrance in advanced and pedimented bay replaced by lumpy balcony. Two-storey wings, c.1830, William Burn, flank central block with Venetian windows. Semicircular stair to rear. Latterly restaurant, now being converted to flats. **Doocot**, 1814, rectangular with gothic details. **Meadowbank**, extensive and idyllic former home farm.

St Margaret's House, St Margaret's Crescent, 1986, Borthwick & Watson
Church of Scotland Sheltered Housing, attractive elongated block, on banked edge of Gray-Buchanan Park, with red-tile roof over red brick and roughcast, pyramid roof over central hall. Terraced gardens to south, link bridge to park to north.

Polmont House, 17th century (demolished 1970s)
Of the three-storey mansion built for Gilbert Laurie, former Lord Provost of Edinburgh, no trace remains except stately avenue of beech trees, transplanted gateposts and marooned early 19th-century Doric **lodge**.

St Margaret's Primary School, 1977,
Central Regional Council Architectural Services
Ingenious quadrangular complex of sculptural two-storey pavilions, slate-clad first floors canted and projected over roughcast ground floors, patent glazing linking all together (see similar school at Bainsford, p.28).

LAURIESTON

One of William Cadell's nail-making centres in the 1770s, Laurieston was feued in 1756 by Francis, 6th Lord Napier, who owned the Merchiston estates in Edinburgh, as a planned urban settlement between Falkirk and Polmont, its original name being New Merchiston. Sold to Sir Laurence Dundas in 1765, the instigator of the Forth & Clyde Canal, hence the present name.

St Mary's Square, a few square feet of trees, seats and greenery focused on **Tam Bain's Public House**, 1910, with domed corner tower, and **Masonic Building**, plaque dated 1870, on north side. Polmont Road today is a hotch-potch of buildings, including **Mecca Bookmakers**, in chunky stonework with a tag-end of exuberant cable hoodmoulding over window and arched doorway, and **Lawries's Public House**, with aggressively corbelled brickwork to mansarded windows.

Top *St Mary's Square and Tam Bain's Public House*. Above *Laurieston Church of Scotland*.

Laurieston Church of Scotland, 1893, A & W Black
Simple gothic buttressed kirk in stone. Belfry to rear and hoodmoulded four-light window to gable.

Laurieston House, 2 Polmont Road, 1850s
Handsome two-storey, three-bay Georgian villa with channelled ground-floor stonework and cast-iron balcony above Doric porch, entered through lintelled gate pillars.

Polmont Road
Plays host to wide variety of house types: **No 4**, white-painted 1960s' bungalow with keyhole porch contrasting with Victorian cottages, their roofs bulging with dormers. Approaching Falkirk, houses become grander, **Norwood** and **Birchbank**, 1890s a delightful pair with filigree ironwork over semicircular bays with round-headed windows.

One of the major employers for the village in later years was the Nobel Factory in Westquarter. Established in 1876, the factory produced detonators for a variety of uses, both commercial and military. Many young women from Laurieston worked there and it was not unusual for homes to contain examples of work done at the factory – grenades without detonators or explosives graced many a mantelpiece. Alfred Nobel is reputed to have stayed at 1 Main Street, when establishing the factory.

Below *Laurieston House*.
Bottom *Norwood and Birchbank*.

Mumrills
East of Laurieston, site of what was once the largest known Roman fort on the Antonine Wall. Some 6½ acres, probably for a cavalry regiment, it stood on an escarpment 100ft above sea level, and contained large headquarters building or *principia*, two granaries, unusually elaborate commandant's house or *praetorium* with private bathing establishment as at Camelon and separate bathhouse for soldiers. Finally abandoned late 2nd century AD. Roman tile- or

brick-making kiln found behind wall. Large civil settlement (*vicus*) in fortified four-acre annexe to south west. Although no traces remain today, coins, pottery and inscribed stones were found during Sir George Macdonald's excavations of 1923–8.

WESTQUARTER

Surrounded by stone wall and situated in its own natural and well-wooded amphitheatre around the Westquarter Burn lie the Westquarter estates, which at the time of the Livingstons amounted to some 300 acres.

Right *Mid-17th century Westquarter House.* Above *Doocot.*

With the decline of the coal industry in central Scotland, particularly in Standburn and Redding, it was decided to house the inhabitants of these villages at Westquarter, whose 63 acres had been bought by the County Council in the 1930s with funds provided under the terms of the Scottish Housing Act of 1935. Such was the novelty and excitement of the proposals at Westquarter that a scale model of the development was exhibited at the Empire Exhibition at Bellahouston Park in 1936.

Westquarter Model Village.

Westquarter House, 1883 (demolished 1934) For Thomas Fenton Livingston, Scots baronial development of original mid-17th-century house for Sir William Livingston. Rectangular lectern **doocot**, 17th century remains, in stone with pronounced stringcourse, scalloped and crowstepped parapets. Livingston arms above doorway.
Guardianship Monument

Westquarter Model Village, 1935–8, John A W Grant Stylistically Arts & Crafts, built for Standburn miners and their families, houses are laid out in

terraced and semidetached groups; curving road patterns enclose greens among trees of the old estate. Set informally on either side of the burn, village comprises 450 predominantly two-storey houses in white render with red-tile roofs, and terraced houses on curving streets. In spite of some vandalism, the scheme proves how successful a simple vocabulary of design elements can be when rigorously adhered to.

John A W Grant, 1885–1959, designed West Muirhouse estate and Foutainbridge Library, both Edinburgh and many 'old Scots' housing developments from 1930–59. Westquarter won the first Saltire Society Housing Design Award in 1937.

Left and above *Westquarter School.*

56 **Westquarter School**, 1939, John A W Grant Symmetrical two-storey in white render, stone trimmings and red slate pavilion roofs with two generous single-storey semicircular bays and very large windows throughout making this a true child of the Modern Movement. Giving expression to contemporary ideas on education, it was a huge step forward from the usual, rather grim schools with their forbidding appearance and acres of hard play areas. The jewel in Westquarter's crown. Saltire Society Architectural Commendation, 1938.

In 1842 large numbers of children were still working in dreadful conditions in collieries all over the east of Scotland, as at Redding which employed 60 children under 13. Margaret Hipps was 17: *she drags a bogie weighing 230 to 350 pounds along a passage 26-28 inches high…It is almost incredible to believe that human beings can submit to such employment, crawling on hands and knees, harnessed like horses, and over soft, slushy floors.*
Calatria, No4

Redding Colliery was owned by James Nimmo and Company, who leased the land from the 13th Duke of Hamilton. The Duke owned the mineral rights to the entire Redding coalfield as well as that of Kinneil and the surrounding area. *At 5am on Tuesday 25 September 1923, a wall in the Dublin section of the main coal seam in No 23 pit gave way and a torrent of water flooded in. Sixty- six men were entombed for nine days and by the 3rd of December 40 bodies had been removed (The Redding Pit Disaster by Amanda Jackson).* Redding Colliery was closed by the National Coal Board in May 1958.

REDDING
South east of Westquarter, small mining community which will unfortunately always be connected with one of Scotland's worst pit disasters in which 40 men lost their lives. Simple **memorial stone**, 1980, at Redding Cross commemorates the event.

Redding & Westquarter Church of Scotland, 1907 Simple gothic kirk with entrance in squat corner tower capped by splayed and slated spire, its church hall to be found in Westquarter.

South of the Union Canal, Brightons, Rumford and Maddiston are strung out along the B805 as it climbs to the moors. All grew up as mining villages, providing much-needed housing for the miners and workers in the new industries. Little of this survives, what remains now swamped by Victorian and modern housing developments.

Redding & Westquarter Church of Scotland.

Top *Church of Scotland.*
Above *Scottish Prison Service College.*

BRIGHTONS
Victorian villas in Main Street and Quarry Brae overlook green expanses of Laurie Park Recreation Centre. **Station Road**, leading to Quarry Brae over the canal bridge, cosy and tree lined (see p.4).

Church of Scotland, 1847, Brown & Carrick
T-plan gothic with pedimented and louvred belfry in well-modelled, pinnacled and buttressed façade; church, with pencil-thin pointed windows, links to modern flat-roofed grey brick and roughcast hall extension. Within church, **stained glass**, 1993, Ruth Golliways.

Harlow Grange, early 20th century
Edwardian villa in roughcast and soft red sandstone; hexagonal corner bay, square porch and semicircular bay giving onto its garden.

Scottish Prison Service College, 1960s
Flat-roofed, spick-and-span white roughcast and horizontally boarded fascia to single-storey block to front, dark brick and panels to three-storey block behind.

HM Young Offenders' Institution, 1911 onwards
Dominated by two four-storey dormered blocks in institutional classic, each with token central pediment, extensive complex in 40-acre grounds utilising original 1888 buildings of Blair Lodge School, just south of the canal.

Blair Lodge Academy, 1888
Only an echo of what was once one of Scotland's top private boarding schools, closed 1904, school being an extension of Blair Lodge House, a pavilion-roofed and porticoed Georgian house of the 1850s.

Blair Lodge Academy was founded in 1838 by the Revd John Cunningham as a private boarding school and expanded to house over 300 boys until 1904, when the company running the school failed and it closed. It was bought by the Prison Commissioners in 1908 and in December of that year the first boys arrived at Polmont Borstal Institution, subsequently Polmont Young Offenders Institution.

The school, which this year celebrates its jubilee… for many years held a high position among the educational establishments in Scotland; but when the present principal came to it in 1874, it was in a deplorably low condition, and there were only seven pupils on its rolls. Mr Gray, formerly an assistant master in Loretto School, brought to bear on his work the wide culture, the stern determination to raise the moral tone. The grounds extend to 40 acres and contain a fine sanatorium and lawn tennis courts. The buildings are sheltered from the cold east winds by belts of timber and the sweet fresh air blowing off Redding Muir is bracing and healthful to a marked degree.
Mr John Anderson, 1888

Blair Lodge Academy.

Blair's Cottages, 1930s
Row of four Arts & Crafts-inspired cottages with
hipped gable dormer details in swept and slated
roof tucked in at the side of the main road.

Braes High School, Newlands Road, 2000,
The Parr Partnership
Crisply designed new school for 1,000 pupils, on
ridge with striking views to north and south,
warningly opposite Young Offenders' Institution.
Lengthy three-storey teaching block with split-
section clerestory aluminium roof and ship's
prow gable to east, parallel to Newlands Road.
Administration, entrance and communal facilities
to south, bordering Polmont Burn. See sister
schools at Falkirk, Bo'ness and Larbert (see pp.30,
59 & 149).

REDDINGMUIRHEAD
South of the canal, Victorian and modern cottages
vie with each other as the road climbs towards
Redding Muir, site of the first Falkirk Trysts,
1707–70s.

Red House Furniture Centre, 1920s
Industrial baroque, large and symmetrical
three-gable red brick warehouse of former
Redding Co-op, with stone insertions including
clasped-hands trade emblem in decorated
centre gable.

Community Centre, Shieldhill Road, 1910
As if hiding behind screen of trees, characterful
single-storey five-bay stone former primary
school, 1856, with his-and-her entrance porches,
former with belfry. Approached through stone
pillars capped with huge stone *peeries*. Built as
school by Duke of Hamilton to serve Redding
Colliery; opened as community centre, 1910, to
provide reading room, billiard room, recreation
room, hall, shooting gallery and bowling green.

From top *Blair's Cottages; Braes High
School; Community Centre; Methodist
Church.*

Methodist Church, Shieldhill Road, 1873
Distinguished less-is-more exercise in narrow
coursed ashlar with gabled frontage, porch,
bullseye window and minuscule belfry.

WALLACESTONE
Wallacestone Monument, 1810
Simple square pillar in public park, with
panoramic views over Falkirk, Grangemouth
and beyond, bearing the inscription: *Erected to
the memory of that celebrated Scottish hero Sir
William Wallace.*

The jury is still out and likely to remain
so on the exact site of the battle of First
Battle of Falkirk, 1298. The general facts
of the battle itself are that Edward I,
'Hammer of the Scots', mustered a force
of some 25,000 infantry and cavalry and
after passing the preceding night in the
area of Linlithgow, engaged the Scots
with a slightly lesser force in two
cavalry charges but failed to dislodge
them from their position. It was only
when the English archers took over that
the tide of the battle turned in their
favour. The Scots were routed, Sir John
de Graeme, Wallace's right hand man
being killed along with 2,000 men.
Wallace himself fled to the sanctuary of
the Tor Wood.

RUMFORD
St Anthony's Polmont, South Craigs Road, 1891
Stone kirk, by picturesque bend in Gardrum Burn,
with dramatic swept tabling to gable, open
timber-framed and slated belfry ingeniously
slotted into parapet of neatly modelled and
advanced tower, added 1919. Now builder's store.

St Anthony's RC Church, Maddiston Road, 1985
Square brick and roughcast church, set back amid
greenery, with slated pyramid roof. Fine interior,
laminated timber beams spanning central space,
stained-glass roundels, black marble altar and
strongly modelled bronze *Stations of the Cross* by
Vincent Butler.

Craig's Terrace, 1940s
Three white-rendered red-tiled terrace blocks,
centre one with wallhead pediments, give well
thought-out feeling to this part of the village.

Compthall and **Prospect House** offer contrasting
styles of 19th-century vernacular in Sunnyside
Road; former, with finialed dormers in white
render and black trim, latter in stone. **Arneil
Place**, 1990s, formed from grounds of Prospect
House, small group of 'executive' bungalows in
red brick and tile. Good landscaping and road
details make this scheme above average.

Top *St Anthony's Polmont*. Middle Stations
of the Cross *by Vincent Butler*. Above
Craig's Terrace.

William Burke, the notorious 19th-
century resurrectionist and murderer,
lived at Maddiston while employed as
a labourer on the Union Canal. His
partner in crime, William Hare, was
living at that time just to the south at
the hamlet known as 'The Loan'.
Calatria, No 7.

The small farm of Whiterigg south of
Maddiston gives scant evidence of the
historical importance of this area. In 1524
King James V, while still in his minority,
granted to Sir James Hamilton of Finnart,
the so-called 'Bastard of Arran', the lands
and barony of Cambusnethan in
Lanarkshire and the lands of Whiterigg
in Stirlingshire, which John Redbag had
forfeited for rebellion against the crown.
In 1539, as a reward for his services in
connection with the building of the royal
palaces of Stirling and Linlithgow (see
Stirling and the Trossachs and *West Lothian*
in this series), Sir James was granted the
much enhanced and enlarged barony
of Avondale.

Maddiston School.

MADDISTON
Largest of the mining villages, it owed its existence
to the rich seams of coal and ironstone, which it
supplied to the Carron Iron Company. Now
sprawling community with pleasant walks by the
Manuel Burn. In **Eccles Place**, tiny modern cottages,
white rendered with black window surrounds.

Cairneymount Church, Main Street, 1904,
James Strang
Strongly modelled stone, with apse and vestry, at
the top of the hill, belfry tower to south, twin
lancets to front gable. **Manse**, 1987, set back, in
buff brick and slates.

Maddiston School, 1912
Characterful single storey in stone and slates
presenting twin gables to road.

Police Station, 1987,
Central Regional Council Architectural Services
Sculptural semicircular flight of steps leads to
deep-silled single storey in dark variegated brick
with slated pavilion roof. **Fire Service HQ**, 1984,
Central Regional Council Architectural Services,
large flat-roofed roughcast block with separate
curved stairtower and lofty tripod aerial above.

MUIRAVONSIDE

Undulating and picturesque, the medieval parish
of Muiravonside is situated at the extreme east of
the district. Criss-crossed by road, rail and canal
with, as focus, the gorge of the river Avon and
the beautiful estate of Muiravonside, now
country park.

57 **Almond (Haining) Castle**, from 14th century,
additions 1586
Ruin of four-storey, L-plan tower in truly
cyclopean masonry, south of Haining Wood, with
vaulted ground and top storeys, chapel on
second floor. Built by the Crawfords; later
acquired by the Livingstons of Callendar who
added shallow twin rectangular-towered
entrance forework (only traces remain) and
changed the name to Almond when they were
elevated to the peerage. Now marooned in
Hepworth's Pipeworks, castle originally
approached by bridge to the south.

Myrehead Farm, late 18th/early 19th century
Farm with ruin of tapering circular windmill tower
some 40ft high and 20ft wide, north of railway.

Muiravonside Parish Church, 1806
Harled, barn-like kirk, in idyllic enclave beside
the canal, with tall pointed windows, wooden
mullions and transoms and painted margins,

In pastoral Scotland, fundamental to the
life of the people was the breeding and
movement of livestock. The latter was to
be ensured by the huge network of so-
called drove roads that by the 17th century
fanned out all over Scotland. South of the
Forth, however, the picture was somewhat
different. Here a virtually single conduit,
serving as a link between Scotland and
England, led from Falkirk, whose tryst was
first held at Reddingsrigg [Redding Muir],
south of Polmont, in a south-easterly
direction through Linlithgow and Bathgate
to Mid Calder and then by way of the
Cauldstane Slap in the Pentlands to
Peebles and the South.

In his description of the parish of
Morvenside (Muiravonside), written
c.1723, Alexander Johnstoun mentions
the crossing of the Avon at the Bridge of
Dalquhairn by 'the Highland cattle from
the markits at Falkirk on their way to the
Borders of England'.

The drove roads were to operate in
one form or another until the early years
of the 19th century until the coming of
the railways.
A R B Haldane, *The Drove Roads of Scotland*

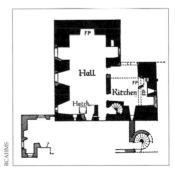

Above *Ground-floor plan, Almond Castle.*
Left *Almond Castle from east.*

Almond Castle
After forfeiture by the 4th Earl of
Callendar in 1716, the castle together
with other properties in the
neighbourhood was acquired by the
York Building Co. in 1720.

Right *Muiravonside Parish Church*.
Above *Decorative tombstone, date
indecipherable, depicting a Quarryman at
work, wielding a hammer, Muiravonside
churchyard. Also to be found, burial
enclosures of many notables including the
Pearsons of Vellore, the Stirlings of Tarduf
House and the Mackenzies of Craigend.*

corbelled belfry with ball finials; Adamesque
ceiling. Until 1947, horseshoe gallery round
'preaching kirk' pulpit in centre of south side.
Stained-glass windows within; bell, 1699, by John
Meikle. Vestibule, vestry and session house, 1947.

Gilmeadowland, early 19th century
Characterful stone farmstead straddling road, its
three-chimneyed, two-storey farmhouse entered
from hipped roof porch. Set into porch wall, small
heraldic panel charged for Livingston, said to be
from Almond Castle and dated 1586.

Avonmuir House, early 19th century
Handsome bay-windowed former manse with
heraldic fragments set in garden.

Below *The Haining*. Bottom *Vellore*.

The Haining, 1825
(?)James Gillespie Graham
Large grey ashlar, two-storey villa, formerly
Parkhall, in established gardens at end of long
drive. Handsome portico with four Doric
columns, piended slate roof; courtyard to rear.

Vellore, from mid-18th century,
(?)James Gillespie Graham
Quixotic Gothick villa, predominantly 1790s,
rectangular plan, two storey, three bay,
symmetrical, with battlements, turrets, matching
porch and drum tower with pepper-pot roof;
19th-century interiors survive. Named after a
massacre in the Indian Mutiny, 1857.

In **1469** Queen Marie, consort of James
II, sold the farms of Compston and
Manuelrig, previously in the possession
of Lord Somerville, to help pay for the
building of the Collegiate Church of the
Holy Trinity (see *Edinburgh* in this
series). In 1590 Timothy Pont considered
it to be of sufficient importance to
denote it on his map, but uses the form
'Cumstown'. At a much later date, the
illustrious Dalzells of the Binns became
associated with Compston.

Easter Manuel Farm
Includes splendid early 19th-century horse-mill.
Tarduf House, mid/late 19th century

Large two-and-a-half-storey mansion, at end of shallow curving drive and among estate trees and rhododendrons, comprising west wing in rubble with banded windows and bay window to gable, projecting east wing having three-light windows to gable at first floor, possibly David Bryce additions to an earlier house. On site of Greenknowes, former home of Walter Gibson, laird of Greenknowes, 1717–1800.

Muiravonside Country Park, The Loan, nr Whitecross
170 acres of woodlands, parklands and garden, including vertiginous slopes abutting the Avon Gorge, now in the care of Falkirk Council. Created from the estate of **Muiravonside House**, U-plan, 17th-century house (demolished 1970s), its foundations may be seen below the old crowstepped home farm, now the visitors' centre.
Lectern **doocot**, 19th-century rebuild of the original, with crowsteps, dormer entries and stringcourse, and a gothic **summerhouse** is tucked into the banking nearby. **Newparks Farm**, former estate manager's house and courtyard, is now developed as a children's farm.
Guidebook

Compston, 18th century
Opposite entrance to country park, two-storey stone farmhouse with fine doorpiece.

Firdale Cottage, 1974, G Paterson
Magical transformation of canal worker's cottage into split-level dream home, with glazed prow, for his family, in idyllic surroundings, affording sensational views of the Avon Aqueduct and Cockleroi.

Manuel House, 1840s, (?)Thomas Hamilton
Baronial two-storey, asymmetrical villa, on

Tarduf House.

Muiravonside Estate, founded in the 12th century by Reginald de Tinsdale, was passed first to the Ross and then to the McLeod families in 1471 and 1724 respectively. It was the Stirlings however and particularly Sir Charles Stirling, who in the 1830s developed the self-sufficient estate which is remembered today, building limekilns, sawmills and overseeing Muiravonside Colliery. As well as their work at Muiravonside the Stirlings were well-known adventurers helping in later years, for instance, to found the SAS, among other worthy endeavours.
The construction of the Slammanan to Bo'ness railway in the 1840s with its stops at Causewayend and Whitecross considerably reduced the area's comparative isolation and even gave rise to an iron foundry near Almond.

From top *Muiravonside Country Park Visitor Centre; Compston; Easter Manuel Farm; Firdale Cottage.*

commanding site overlooking the Avon, presenting three gables to main front. Tower with pepper-pot roof, bay windows to gardens, Tudor **lodge**.

Manuel Mill House, late 18th century
Good plain rubble and slate two-storey farmhouse with courtyard. **Manuel Mill**, late 18th/early 19th century, unusually extensive rubble ashlar corn mill with huge arched opening for farm machinery; impressive lade system from River Avon.

Manuel Nunnery, 1731 drawing.

RCAHMS

58 **Manuel Nunnery**, 12th century
Buttressed fragment only of Cistercian nunnery founded by Malcolm IV, on the banks of the Avon, which has altered its course considerably over the years. Drawing of 1731 in Bodleian Library shows plain roofless rectangular building with one circular and three pointed windows in the extant gable.

Manuel Nunnery
Edward III recompensed the convent for damage caused by his army on its march towards Leith in the summer of 1335. In 1506 a petition of James IV for the suppression of the house, on the grounds that the nuns were scarcely five in number and led a life alien to the Cistercian rule, was granted, but not put into effect as a prioress and four nuns were still resident in 1552.

The extent of Manuel's holdings within central Scotland is not known. The house was not a wealthy one and its possessions were probably few and in no way comparable to that at Newbattle in Midlothian (see *Midlothian* in this series), which held extensive lands in the carse of Falkirk as well as many saltpans. Similar Cistercian houses to Manuel were founded at the same period in Haddington and North Berwick.

Canal craft, or scows, were built of iron and pulled by one horse, larger boats, lighters, being pulled by two. Distances are marked by mile posts and the whole length is divided into four stages for dues.

Union Canal, 1822, Hugh Baird
Some 30 miles long, the canal, connecting Edinburgh to Falkirk, was built to provide a route for supplying coal, sandstone, slate and granite cobbles to the rapidly developing New Town of Edinburgh. Connected to Forth & Clyde Canal at Lock 16 at Camelon, it flourished for nearly 20 years when its function was taken over by the Edinburgh & Glasgow Railway which arrived in 1842. The canal survived in part but the Edinburgh basins closed in 1922, the lock flight at Camelon in 1933 and the whole system in 1965.

Today, as part of British Waterways' £78m Millennium Link project, the Union Canal, together with the Forth & Clyde Canal, has been given a new lease of life as a national recreational and leisure facility. A major feature of the Union Canal is the three huge aqueducts over the Almond, Water of Leith and the Avon, all three grandly picturesque and redolent of that great age of engineering.

Jaques

The trough of the **Avon Aqueduct**, like the others over the River Almond and the Water of Leith, is cast iron rather than stone lined with puddle clay. As a consequence the supporting piers did not require to be filled with rubble but have hollow walls strengthened by internal braces.

Avon Aqueduct. Below *Candie House*. Middle *Candiehead*. Bottom *Drawing room, Lathallan*.

Marshall Wilson

Susan Skinner

Joe Rock

Avon Aqueduct, 1820, Hugh Baird
Supported by 12 arches, 810ft long, it carries the Union Canal across the steep-sided Avon Valley, 85ft above river level. Truly majestic and one of the finest in the UK. Near the aqueduct is the old Slamannan Railway basin, a small dry dock and Scotland's only surviving canal tunnel at Prospect Hill, south of Falkirk.

Candie House, early 1800s
White-rendered L-plan house, plain but dignified high up in wooded estate near Standburn. Doorway with entablature. Currently being restored with extension replaced. **Candiehead**, pretty stone cottage with timber gabled porch, dormers and oculus.

Lathallan, 1826–8, Thomas Hamilton
Former Laurence Park House, at end of long estate drive, twin gables flanking central porch. Pepper-pot tower in angle, large mullioned windows and hoodmoulds, grouped octagonal chimneys; stable block adjoins. Derelict and at serious risk, fine interiors including panelled library, plasterwork to ceilings and rib-vaulting to bay windows, all vandalised.

SHIELDHILL

Mining community established by the Carron Iron Company on former Hamilton lands and one of the earliest Tryst sites. Situated 500ft above sea level on a ridge between Reddingmuirhead and Slamannan, it gives breathtaking views of Forth Valley to north, bleak expanses of Gardrum Moss and Loch Ellrig to the south.

Raws, or rows of miners' houses and two-storey pit manager's house long disappeared.

The prevailing system of agriculture in Scotland in the late 18th century, had many aspects relating it to that in Scandinavia. The Norse settlers who introduced the method of farming were largely dependant on a pastoral economy and so larger areas of pasture were required than was normally available as part of a farm unit.

In the summer herds were taken to remote and unsettled moors for larger pasturage and where temporary huts, 'sheilings' were built. Evidence suggests Shieldhill had been such a settlement. From *Shieldhill – A Glimpse of the Past*, Falkirk District Council Libraries and Museums

Blackbraes & Shieldhill Parish Church, 1864
T-plan stone former United Free Church, built by
Revd Lewis H Irving, minister; enlarged, 1894.
Red tiled roof with three slim lancet windows,
slender belfry to gable and gallery within (see
also Irving Church of Scotland, p.46).

Greenmount, Duncan's Farm, 1810
Cosily proportioned dormered block with
banded windows, originally part of large dairy
farm, complete with stabling for horses. Chimney
detail suggests roof thatched previously.

CALIFORNIA
Not quite like its sun-drenched namesake, a tiny
mining community high upon the moors west of
Wallacestone comprising Church Road – church
gone but handsome two-storey stone manse
Seaforth, 1896, remains – and Princes Street.

AVONBRIDGE
Mining community to south east, in a beautiful
situation at a crossing of the River Avon.

Avonbridge Parish Church of Scotland, 1890,
A & W Black
Gothic, in stone and slates with buttressed porch,
hoodmoulded rose window and belfry. Built for
the followers of the Revd James Morrison and Mr
Rutherford, the latter being expelled from the
United Secession Church for telling of its 'soul-
ruining doctrines'.

*Below Avonbridge Parish Church of
Scotland. Bottom Greyrigg Inn.*

Linn Mill, c.1860
Handsome rubble group backing on to the
hillside, house with ashlar quoins and dressings
to doors and windows, stable block with arched
opening and steps to gable entrance.

Greyrigg Inn
Distinctive white rendered hostelry with black-
painted quoins and window surrounds and horse
and carriage mural on gable on bleak stretch of
moorland road between California and Slamannan.
Clearly from its size, an important stop-over on
what was the drove road from Cauldstane Slap via
Bathgate to Falkirk and beyond.

Loch Ellrig
Lonely grey sliver of water on the fringes of the
Gardrum Moss, a bleak and largely treeless area of
moorland. Clumps of reeds, broom, buttercups and
bog-cotton, together with the cry of the peewit,
give it a special beauty of its own (see colour p.87).

Ellrig House (demolished 1999)
Romantic ruin south of Loch Ellrig, in large
sloping and wooded estate, former home of John
B Ralston. Two-storey mansion with Ionic
doorpiece, linking three-storey battlemented
tower and courtyard. Surviving gothic **lodge**,
L-plan, in stone with fine scrolled skewputts,
bullseye window in gable to driveway.

SLAMANNAN
Ancient community dating back at least to the
12th century, developed in the 19th century, south
of Falkirk, around the coal industry. Lying high
up in the moors at a natural crossroads and at a
loop in the Culloch Burn, it is surrounded by
open country where every winter flocks of the
rare bean goose stop on their migration south.

The **Slamannan Railway**, opened 1840s, was one
of the earliest public railways in Scotland.
Connecting the mining communities of the moors
to the dock on the Union Canal, it was later
extended to Bo'ness.

Top *Ellrig House.* Above *Lodge, Ellrig House.* Left *Parish Church of St Lawrence.*

As the railways grew from short-term
feeders for the canal system to become
an alternative means of transport in the
1830s–40s, a great boom in construction,
'Railway Mania' took place. The first
line to cross the Falkirk area, the
Slammanan Railway, was conceived as a
way of bringing Monklands coal via the
Union Canal to Edinburgh. It was
opened on 31 August 1840 and ran for
12½ miles from Airdriehill to
Causewayend coal basin where loads
were taken onto canal barges.
The railways had a huge impact on
social as well as commercial life, one
result being the regular trips taken to
Airdrie by the previously isolated
villagers of the Slammanan plateau.

Parish Church of St Lawrence, 1810
On a raised knoll with surrounding cemetery, in
rubble and slates, simple domestic-scaled
building with wide-awake presence, the result of
good proportions and disposition of the tall
banded windows. Belfreyed gable with 1722
Maxwell bell; gallery within (see p.4). Remains of
small **sundial** and tiny, separate **session house**.

Motte, 12th century
Raised mound north of the church all that
remains of medieval motte and bailey. Excellent
views of village and surrounding countryside.

From top *Ladysland; Thorndene Terrace; St Mary's Chapel.*

Church Hall, 1901
In rubble, with crowstepped gable, distinguished by large hoodmoulded windows.

Ladysland, *c.*1890s
Beautifully crafted cottage, on corner site, with pedimented dormers and porch.

Thorndene Terrace, 1981, Kennedy Partnership
Well-planned group, for Hanover Housing Association, in white roughcast and grey tiles with glazed entrance links.

Royal Hotel, 1866
Natural focus of town centre, in white render with black cornice banding, window surrounds and piended slate roof.

War Memorial, 1921 and 1949
Three noble and bewhiskered sandstone lions guard a quiet corner of High Street containing polished pink marble memorial to First and Second World Wars against leafy background.

Waddel Monument, 1902, J M Dick Peddie, Joseph Hayes, sculptor
Ornate column, with exquisitely carved capital of birds in foliage, bearing clock by Barrie's of Edinburgh and obelisk crown. A plaque records: *In memory of George Ralston Peddie Waddel of Balquhatstone, died 1901, in the Transvaal, aged 26 years.*

St Mary's Chapel, Bank Street, 1960
Simple statement in roughcast, timber and felted pitched roof has homely appeal with its generous porch, simple buttressing; small, DIY spire, now no more.

59 **Balquhatstone House**, 1871, John Dick Peddie
T-shaped mansion in extensive grounds, for the architect's brother, built around earlier house. Principal frontage distinguished by long pillared

Balquhatstone House.

porch and single-storey bay to projecting gable; the composition now confused by later three-storey bay-window addition. Service yard and offices with doocot over entrance pend. **Lodge**, 1852.

Pirnie Lodge, 1735
Simple two-storey house with crowstepped gables, marriage lintel over central doorway: *MR W H & I S 1735* (William Hastie and Isabella Shaw). Extended 1867.

LIMERIGG
Despite the name, another community that owed its existence to the coal industry. At the edge of moorland but completely contained within the magnificent dark evergreens of Limerigg Wood (now managed by Forest Enterprise), it has something of a frontier feel to it. Take the road from Limerigg to Avonbridge, along a ridge with some beautiful countryside and ever-changing views to north and south.

Parish Church, 1950s
Underlining the frontier feel, *Waltons'*-style House of God in cream render with lancet windows, stained timber frontage, porch and corrugated roofing.

Black Loch
Beyond the village, the road to Avonbridge skirts the generous expanse of the **Black Loch**, a deservedly popular centre for fishing and water sports. **Loch House**, 1900s, two-storey farmhouse guarded by remarkable concrete sheep on the front lawn.

GRANGEMOUTH
Derives its name from the Grange Burn, which at one time snaked around the grange or *ferme* and emptied itself into the River Carron. Lying almost at sea level, the tree-covered slopes of the 50ft raised glacial beach behind, acting as spectacular backdrop. Now a centre for oil refining and chemical manufacturing, ancient farms and spreading fields of wheat in the Carselands contrast surreally with the huge geometries of cooling towers and flare stacks.

The modern town, now reached by a generous motorway system is almost Gallic in character with its gridiron plan and wide leafy boulevards as if Haussmann or Craig had come to town. Today, whilst the oil and chemical industries have proved to be a mixed blessing, Grangemouth is a thriving community.

Top *Limerigg Parish Church.*
Above *Loch House.*

Rising in the Kilsyth Hills and feeding the Carron Valley Reservoir, the **River Carron** travels 20 miles before disgorging into the Forth at Grangemouth. *This River, famed in Celtic antiquities, and rendered classic from its connection with incidents in Scottish history, takes its rise in the central parts of the county. It flows in an easterly direction with a sinuous course for about fourteen miles, and joins the Forth a little below the Port of Grangemouth. In full tide, it is navigable for vessels of 20 tons burden, as far as Carronshore, which may be two miles from its embouchure. Above this it is a transparent stream and abounds with trout, perch, eels etc., but further down it has a muddy bed, by which the water is discoloured. It seeks its way to the Forth through a deposit of the richest alluvial matter.*
The Second Statistical Account of Falkirk, 1845

Grangemouth, 1854.

Top *Canal Street, c.1900.* Above *Doorway detail, South Basin Street.*

60 Old Town, *c.*1768

Founded by the Dundas family, Sir Laurence Dundas purchasing Kerse House from the Hope family in 1752. He foresaw the advantages to be gained by developing a port at the point where the Forth & Clyde Canal entered the Forth and began the building programme which was to be continued by his son, Sir Thomas Dundas. For most of the 19th century until the creation of the Burgh of Grangemouth in 1872, the family continued to exert a leading influence on the affairs and development of the town. Maritime trade was the foundation on which the town grew, exporting the produce of the area's industries both along the Forth and west through the Forth & Clyde Canal. The traditional trade of east-coast ports with the Baltic was continued by

South Bridge Street, c.1890s.

An observer some time after Grangemouth's heyday writes: *The Old Town is the more picturesque part of the port. It is married to the water like a second Venice, but a Venice of the north with quaint grey-stone buildings jostling with wharves, boatslips, workshops, inns with a nautical flavour, warehouses and timber basins. It is a crowded place, but has enchanting vistas down old-fashioned streets and lanes, abutting in waterways where sea-fowl float and disturb the placid reflections of the houses of the wealthy merchants of the last century, whose nobly proportioned rooms have long since been converted to other purposes.*

Grangemouth and Scandinavian timber was a major import.

The first Grangemouth, the Old Town, grew between the River Carron and the Grange Burn as a direct result of the building of the Forth & Clyde Canal which brought new trade up the river. With this growth in trade came the need for bigger port facilities and soon Grangemouth overtook Carronshore and then Bo'ness in the amount of trade handled; a custom house was erected in North Harbour Street.

Sir Laurence Dundas planned the original town (known as Sea Lock or Grange Burn Mouth) as a model one with broad gridded streets and regular frontages. While the homes were intended for the port's workers rather than the upper classes, they were nevertheless soundly built, many with attractive scroll mouldings to their door surrounds.

It is a pity that today most of the Old Town has been or is being demolished bearing in mind that Grangemouth, for all its successes, has in this respect so little to lose in terms of its heritage and history.

Sir Laurence Dundas, the son of Thomas Dundas, and one-time MP for Linlithgow, amassed a fortune in the service of the Duke of Cumberland. At the close of the Seven Years' War, being made a Baronet he returned to West Kerse which he had purchased in 1752 and not only gave full support for the construction of the Great Canal, but managed to have the position of the terminal altered so that it was built on his recently acquired lands – a neat and profitable reversal of the not-in-my-back-yard philosophy!

Kerse House, from 14th century
Original c.1640 house reconstructed and enlarged, 1830–1, John Tait, to extensive three-storey Jacobean style mansion and estate, home of the Dundas family for nearly 200 years. Demolished 1950s, nothing remains except some brick walling and circular cavity-walled **ice house**.

Old Town Hall, 1876, 25 South Bridge Street
Two-storey, five-bay classical building, three-stage clock tower over central projecting bay. In poor condition, as is **Queen's Hotel**, its grandly pedimented neighbour to the west.

Forth & Clyde Canal, 1768–90, John Smeaton & Robert McKell
Linking Grangemouth with the Clyde at Bowling and designed expressly to facilitate trade, particularly coal and timber, between the Forth

Falkirk Museums

Kerse House was erected by Sir Thomas Hope, Lord Advocate for Scotland in 1642 for his second son, Sir Thomas Hope (Lord Kerse), Lord Justice-General for Scotland. Sir Thomas Sr was the first commoner to be appointed Moderator of the Church of Scotland.

Left *Kerse House.* Below *Old Town Hall.*

RCAHMS

Proposals for a **Forth & Clyde Canal** date back to the reign of Charles II, 100 years earlier, but it was not until the 1760s that surveys were made and John Smeaton appointed as engineer. The first cut was made in 1768 at the eastern sea lock (Grangemouth). By 1777 it had reached Glasgow but work had to stop through lack of funds. In 1784 money raised from the sale of forfeited Jacobite estates allowed the project to be completed, a fact which ties our industrial and national history neatly together. By 1792 ocean to ocean travel was a reality.

Monument to the River Clyde, Robert Adam, 1760s. Inscription reads Dedicated to the River Clyde which joined to the Forth by the Canal between these Rivers unites the influence of both in extending the Wealth and Prosperity of Scotland. *Might have been speculative but more likely a commission had been mooted.*

and the fast-developing town of Glasgow, the 37 miles canal was the catalyst that initiated the development of Sea Lock or Grange Burn Mouth, as the developing hamlet was variously called in its early days. In 1867, the Caledonian Railway bought the canal and port, the passenger service operating until 1967. The large timber basins which formed such a distinctive feature of the port and which are reminiscent of those early photographs of the Canadian rivers were filled in in the 1970s.

The Forth & Clyde Canal finally closed in 1963 after some 170 years of service but, in 2001, the £78m **Millennium Link Project** by British Waterways, is re-opening both the Forth & Clyde and the Union Canals, including the reconnection of the Forth & Clyde Canal with the River Carron at Grangemouth for recreational and amenity purposes.

Above *Charlotte Dundas and Canal.*
Right *Docks.*

The most famous boat built in the town was undoubtedly, the *Charlotte Dundas.* Designed by William Symington, built by Alexander Hart and sponsored by Lord Dundas, it was launched in 1801, 11 years before Henry Bell's *Comet* on the Clyde. The boat was 56ft long, had a beam of 18ft and a horizontal cylinder giving direct drive to a paddle wheel. After only a few years' service on the canal it was withdrawn by the authorities who feared the wash from the paddle would damage its banks. William Symington, who was born at Leadhills in Lanarkshire in 1764, died in penury in London in 1831. The *Charlotte Dundas* is, however, commemorated in the town's coat of arms.

Docks, 1830 onwards
A primary site of Scotland's industrial revolution. Founded by Sir Laurence Dundas of Kerse and built by the Forth & Clyde Canal Company. It was Grange Dock, with its vast 30-acre expanse, that gave the docks, formerly served only by the Carron, an entrance from the Forth. At one time served by road and rail, now a vast network comprising Junction Dock, Grange Dock, Western and Eastern Channels. Original docks now almost totally derelict, save for occasional boating. A squat white lighthouse marks the old entrance at the north east.

Shipyard, late 18th century onwards
Included Alexander Hart's Yard, the birthplace of the *Charlotte Dundas*, the first practical steamship, named after Sir Laurence Dundas' daughter.

Refinery, 1924 onwards
Covering more than a square mile of gridded streets many with numbers only, the complex, started by Scottish Oils and now including a huge chemical manufacturing area, forms today by far the most dominant element of the townscape. By day awesome, with its belching cooling-towers, chemistry-set complexes and burning-off flares, by night a truly spectacular sight, like Gustav Doré's illustrations to Danté's *Inferno* (see colour p.87).

Earl's Road
Avecia
Well-known landmark to all motorists on the M9, this elegant high-tech tower, formerly Zeneca/ICI Chemicals, with its blue and white livery, neat logo and spiralling escape stair sets a high standard for the town's industrial architecture (see colour p.87).

Forrestwood, early 1900s
Handsome two-storey, bay-windowed villa incorporating asymmetrical Art Nouveau entrance panel with semicircular window: coloured glass of the period in its large three-pane stair window. Clearly a manager's house.

Left Grangemouth Refinery. From top Flare drums, KG Plant; Ethylene furnace, KG Plant; the Refinery dominates the townscape; Forrestwood.

BP Social and Recreation Club, Grange Road, 1974, Basil Spence and Partners
Extensive and well-articulated brick box over recessed base, services in metal-clad plant rooms over. Playing fields adjoin.

Mallinson Denny's slatted timber sheds in **Wood Street**, now, alas, demolished, were a fine feature in this part of the town and an echo of one of Grangemouth's principal industries from the 1750s.

West Church, Dalgrain Road, 1837, John Tait (demolished 1980s)
Robust, cruciform, broad shouldered and belfried with the armorial plaque of the Dundas family over its doorway, the first of Grangemouth's nine churches. **Stained-glass windows** rescued from demolition now at Grangemouth Museum.

BP Social and Recreation Club.

Grangemouth Bonding Co. Ltd
Handsome four-storey warehouse in brick, with stone trimmings and windows between giant pilasters.

The Granary, Dalgrain Road, 1817 (demolished)
Three-storey stone warehouse with winch mechanism in gable end, built by the Carron Iron Company.

Thistlebank, Dalgrain Road, 1890s
Scots Baronial villa of zestful extravagance, bristling with crowsteps, corbelled and parapeted corner turrets, the whole tied together at the ground floor with exuberant ropework moulding. There were at least three ropewalks in the area in the early 19th century.

Top *Grangemouth Bonding Co. Ltd.*
Above *Thistlebank.* Right *Charing Cross and Charing Cross Church of Scotland c.1900.*

61 Town Centre and Charing Cross
Disappointing junction between the old and the new, made worse by modern road 'improvements'. Seen in retrospect, the Second Town Plan would have benefited from the provision of a new centre. Only the tiny sooty and pedimented **Royal Bank of Scotland** with its handsome clocktower on the gushet site adds a touch of quiet dignity to the scene. A clean-up for this little building would help to regenerate one's first impressions of the town.

Below *Royal Bank of Scotland.*
Bottom *Caley Bingo.*

Caley Bingo, Station Road, 1939, Alister MacDonald
Alister MacDonald was the architect son of Prime Minister Ramsay. On busy curving corner site, large façade of red brick, stone trim of former La Scala, including cornices and pilasters, the body of the hall clamped between domed towers. The words 'Empire Electric' on entrance pediment behind present logo recall the early excitements of cinema-going.

La Porte Shopping Precinct, 1975,
Wheeler & Sproson
Formerly Lumley Street, prefaced today by the
successful later additions of glazed rotunda and
covered way in attractive Gallic green livery and
named after La Porte, Indiana USA,
Grangemouth's twin town. Old and new
buildings faithfully reflect original axial layout of
the part of the New Town it has replaced.
Pedestrian area with trees, brick paviors and
planters. Of the original Victorian buildings at the
entry to the precinct, George Washington
Browne's excellent brownstone **British Linen
Bank** frontage of the 1890s excels, asymmetrical
under finialed and richly decorated Dutch gables
(see also Bank of Scotland in Falkirk's Vicar
Street, p.23).

62 **Central Area Development**, 1972–6,
Wheeler & Sproson
Arcaded shopping layout, Kerse Road housing
and public buildings. Its rigorous if somewhat
severe layout, intelligent and appropriate use of
artificial stone, roughcast finishes and standard
monopitch-roofed housing combine to make this
an above average scheme for its time and one
which forms an appreciable addition to the town.

Alan Davie Mural, The Square, 1975
Depicting the town and its industries, in
shimmering coloured mosaic, executed by
George Garson. Sponsored by BP Refinery
(Grangemouth) Ltd and BP Chemicals
(International) Ltd. The internationally renowned
artist was born in the town (see colour p.87).

New Town
The Dundas family continued the high standard
of town planning into the New Town starting in
1861 and spreading east from the Canal to the
Grange Burn, using Bo'ness Road as its main
artery. Anticipating the ideas of the Garden
Cities Movement, each home had its garden. In
1872, Grangemouth was granted burgh status
and by 1900 it had a population of 5000, a town
hall, a library and a public park. With the
development of **Bo'ness Road**, the town soon
possessed a wide tree-lined avenue of Victorian
terrace and villa development (including J M
MacLaren's two exceptional villas Avon Hall
and Avon Dhu) linking Old and New Towns
and eventually carving its way through
Oilopolis (the former Bearcroft area) to the east.

From top *La Porte Shopping Precinct;*
Interior, La Porte Shopping Precinct;
British Linen Bank; Central Area
Development.

Grangemouth Town Hall, 1886, A & W Black
Reconstructed in 1938 by Wilson & Wilson.
Dignified, balustraded classical block in coursed
grey ashlar, first-floor windows framed by twin
Corinthian pilasters over channelled ground-
floor masonry. The original railings and lamps
long since gone. Proposals for a very grandiose
Scots Baronial hall incorporating turreted tower
were made by J G Fairley but the Blacks' scheme
was chosen.

Victoria Public Library, 1890, A & W Black
Pinched classical block with round-headed
windows at first floor. Erected at the time of the
Queen's Jubilee with a donation from Andrew
Carnegie, it now includes small exhibition of local
history, including brilliant **stained-glass window**
from West Church, 1893, model of the *Charlotte
Dundas*, and the 'Winged Tiger', sculptural logo
from Grangemouth's short-lived airport.

Top *Grangemouth Town Hall*. Above
Victoria Public Library. Right
Grangemouth Municipal Chambers.

W G Rowan, 1845–1924, never quite
achieved the national reputation his
abilities warranted. A pupil of Sir Charles
Barry's ex-assistant, George Penrose
Kennedy, from 1862–7, he went on to
learn the business of civil engineering
with J F Blair before setting up in
partnership with John McKissack in
Glasgow in 1872. His early works were of
Alexander Thomson inspiration but in
the 1880s he became an exponent of Scots
gothic in parallel with the London Scot J J
Stevenson. By the 1890s he had fallen
under the spell of John Dando Sedding
and Harry Wilson, working in a reformed
free neo-Perpendicular. Craigmailen
United Free Church at Braehead, Bo'ness,
was his first essay in the Scots gothic
genre (see p.140).

Municipal Chambers, 1939, Wilson & Tait
Characterful and well-massed block with
shallow-pitched hipped roof tucked behind
carefully detailed parapet. Creamy sandstone
channelled stonework at ground floor, triple
round-headed windows to council chamber at
first floor; flagpoles for civic pride.

**Charing Cross Church of Scotland and
West Church**, 1884, W G Rowan
Unusual, expressionist and very Nordic former
Zetland Free Church in tawny brown ashlar.
Pinched lancet windows in central tower of
cruciform frontage surge up to steep slated
gables, two corner turrets clamped tightly
between corner buttressing (see p.116).

Bo'ness Road

Starting at the Grange Burn and running straight as a die, due east and west for some 2½ miles, Bo'ness Road, tree-lined and flanked by Victorian terraces and villas, also serves the housing estates to north and south as well as the oil refinery to the east. Near the latter, extraordinary juxtapositions of leafy suburbia and belching cooling towers.

63 **Dundas Church**, 1894, Sir John James Burnet
In rubble with ashlar dressings, superb Romanesque rectangular plan with central arcade, entered by generous timber framed porch. Squat square tower with two louvred lancets and short, slated spire behind corbelled parapet. Beautifully proportioned glazed link terminates in a projecting octagonal vestry. A building of real distinction. Compare similar churches by Burnet at Stenhousemuir (see p.58), Brechin, Lossiemouth and Glasgow (see *District of Moray* and *Central Glasgow* in this series).

Dundas Church.

A letter from Sir John James Burnet to Thomas McGill Esq, 24 March 1893, displayed in **Dundas UP Church** reads: *Dear Sir, I herewith send you 2 schemes A & B of the proposed new church. In design A, I have endeavoured to meet your requirements with a church in which every sitter will have a clear and uninterrupted view of the pulpit, but it would be expensive to construct a church in the mode you propose, i.e. with the possibility of adding a Gallery later on. The feature of the church is the Gallery and it would require to be put in at the beginning. The accommodation would be 636 of which 350 would be in the area and 286 in the Gallery, which taken at £5.15 per sitting (about your limit) would bring the design out at £3657…*

Left *Avon Hall*. Above *Avon Dhu*.

Avon Hall and **Avon Dhu**, 1878, J M MacLaren
The French Connection; superb pair of rubble-built and very Gallic-looking Scots Baronial mansions, the first independent designs by one of Scotland's lesser-known pioneering architects.

Avon Hall

Robustly asymmetrical, for John Fairley, balancing busy verticals of main house, two-storey bays and circular corner entrance drum with low-slung kitchen wing, still enjoying the prospect afforded by its original and superb garden layout. Much intriguing detail; outside, elaborately embellished entrance doorway, square-plan gatepiers and third-floor dormer; inside, circular entrance porch with

James Marjoribanks MacLaren 1853–90, Born in Middleton, Thornhill, and educated at Stirling High School, gained his earliest architectural training with James Salmon I before joining the Glasgow firm headed by Campbell Douglas and J J Stevenson. After the break-up of this partnership Stevenson moved to London setting up on his own. Following the design of his most successful large building, Stirling High School, 1887–8 (see *Stirling & The Trossachs* in this series), he produced a number of remarkable works in Perthshire for his patron Sir Donald Currie of Glenlyon, notably the Tenant Farmer's House and Aberfeldy Town Hall, both 1889–90 (see *Perth & Kinross* in this series).

Sir John Burnet, architect for Grangemouth War Memorial, took everyone, including the monument's committee, by surprise when he produced his design. The completed monument was dominated by a sculptural group portraying the British Lion with its teeth sunk into the German Eagle. The hapless eagle had not featured on any of the architect's original sketches nor was it felt to be in keeping with the prevailing spirit of forgiveness and reconciliation. Attempts were made by certain pressure groups to have the lion's grasp relaxed or the eagle omitted entirely but the designer was adamant that it was an integral part of this composition and his wishes prevailed. Geoff B Bailey, from *Calatria No 6*

War Memorial, Zetland Public Park.

Abbotsgrange
Following the First and Second Charters of King James I in 1429 and 1450 respectively, the lands of the Barony of Kerse (from Abbotsgrange in the east to Carron in the west) were given to Holyrood Abbey. The ancient farmlands, some of which, it is said, had existed before Roman times, were laid out on a scientific basis, measuring their terrains in cottarlands, oxgaits, husbandlands and ploughgaits. The oxgait was what one ox could cultivate *where pleuch and scythe may gang* and was rated around 13 acres. The husbandland equalled 26 acres and the ploughgate the work of four oxen, forming a ferme. Cottars dwelling near the grange had only a few acres of land.

Grange Burn looking north.

coloured glass; elsewhere, original decorated plaster ceilings, fireplaces and furniture. Now a reception centre for guests of BP.

Avon Dhu
Even more Gallic than its neighbour by way of its thrusting boat-shaped bay, decorated and pedimented dormer under steeply pitched pyramid roof and elaborate entrance under richly carved plaque depicting monsters of the deep. Built for woodmill owner Alexander MacLaren for his wife and family. Now converted to flats and marooned in a sea of builder's 'executive' villas.

64 Zetland Public Park and Fountain
Opened in 1882, the park's original 8½ acres now extend to some 50 acres for all forms of recreational use. Both take their names from Grangemouth's benefactor, The Earl of Zetland.

War Memorial, 1919, Sir John James Burnet, Alexander Proudfoot, sculptor
Above a Lutyenesque tapering granite base are depicted the British Lion devouring the German Eagle. Formally designed with gates and ornamental pillars at the entrance to the park, the memorial was the subject of much controversy.

Abbotsgrange
Apart from Kerse, the other great house was that of the Grange of the Abbots of Holyrood which, after the Reformation, passed into the hands of the Bellendens, the Earls of Roxburgh and the Drummonds of Blair Drummond. A **ring of trees** beside the paddling pool is all that remain today to mark the alleged site.

Adjacent to the park, a veritable 'Holy Corner' of some five churches served an equal number of religious faiths.

Grange Burn
One of Grangemouth's three waterways and the one that gave the town its name, its course originally taking a large easterly loop but now carving a virtually straight line in a culvert from Beancross in the south to Bo'ness Road at the north, then east to its mouth north of the refinery. Tree-lined for most of the way it gives a very Dutch feeling to the New Town.

Sacred Heart RC Church, Dalratho Road, 1927, Archibald Macpherson
In Romanesque, the favourite style of this maverick and always-interesting architect. Stone

Jaques

Sacred Heart RC Church.

Archibald Macpherson, 1851–1927, established his own practice in Edinburgh in 1879, works from that time including St Aloysius College in Glasgow, the Chapel of St Catherine's Convent in Edinburgh (see *Central Glasgow* and *Edinburgh* in this series) and Our Lady of Loretto in Musselburgh. However it was his later work in brick, in the churches at Bannockburn, Grangemouth and Rosewell that he was to demonstrate that he was no slave to fashion. Almost childlike and strangely proportioned, each exhibits a sense of thoughtfulness and rigour that overcomes initial doubts.

with red-tiled roof, its slim west gable enlivened by charming arcaded porch below figure of Christ in niche and three tiers of tiny round-headed windows. Inside, walls and round columns in grey brick. (See also Macpherson's unusual churches at Rosewell and Bannockburn in *Midlothian* and *Stirling & The Trossachs* in this series.)

Grange Parish Church, Ronaldshay Crescent/ Park Road, 1903, G Deas Page
On prominent corner site, beefy Arts & Crafts aisled and galleried Church of Scotland, in brown rubble with contrasting quoins and opening surrounds, entered at corner tower, twin lancets to tower under beetling eyebrow hoods and pyramid roof. Converted to flats in 1990s.

Below *Grange Parish Church.* Middle *Zetland Parish Church.* Bottom *St Mary's Episcopal Church.*

65 **Zetland Parish Church**, Old Parish Church, Ronaldshay Crescent, 1906, Wilson & Tait
Asymmetrical Church of Scotland in grey ashlar dominated by brusquely parapeted and perforated tower with pencil-thin moonrocket stairtower and cavernous doorway.

Jaques

St Mary's Episcopal Church, 1937, Maxtone Craig
Simple stone and slate church with round-headed windows entered by porch at south-west corner. Built with the stone from Kerse house.

Kerse Church, Abbot's Road, 1899, J P Goodsir
Very dignified and secluded cruciform group behind the trees and overlooking Zetland Park. In ashlar, with slated roof, entered from porch in its buttressed façade to the north. Pencil-thin mini-spire. Linked **church hall** addition to north, 1930, Henry Wilson.

Grange Primary School, Park Road/Dalratho Road, 1893, G Deas Page
Impressively gabled and finely proportioned red sandstone Jacobean block, planned foursquare

Jaques

around galleried hall with grand staircase. Built as Grange Public School for Grangemouth School Board, demolished 1998.

Abbotsgrange Middle School, Carronflats Road, 1908, Wilson & Tait
Grandly pedimented and well-detailed, classical, two-storey, red sandstone former Grangemouth High School, statuary enlivening central balustraded pediment, separate boys' and girls' entrances. Inside, stained-glass windows, by Meikle, to the two light wells with colonnaded arcading to galleries. Converted to flats, 1990s.

Grangemouth Sports Complex and **Youth and Community Centre**, Abbot's Road, 1971 and 1975 respectively, Wilson & Wilson
Linked leisure facilities including swimming pool and two sports halls in white roughcast and ribbed blue metal fascias, all overlooking the lush landscaping of Zetland Park.

Top Grange School. Above Grangemouth Sports Complex and Youth and Community Centre.

Charlotte Dundas Court, 1970, Philip Cocker & Partners
Pioneering attempt, notwithstanding jostling hotch-potch of incompatible materials, to create multi-use space with shops, housing and a hotel. Subsidence began the slide downhill and vandalism did the rest.

Below YMCA, Abbots Road, two pedimented gables, one to side elevation of offices, the other to hall make for an interesting composition. Middle Pumping Station. Bottom Grangemouth Stadium.

Housing, Kersie Bank Avenue, 1967, Wilson & Wilson
Opposite stadium among trees, pleasantly scaled five-storey blocks of flats and maisonettes.

Pumping Station, 1967, Grangemouth Burgh Council, Baptie, Shaw & Morton (Engineers)
Simple flat-roofed structure, its workings visible through large window and from gallery inside. External alterations and recladding, 2000, Keppie Architects. Grangemouth suffers from the combined problems of a high water-table and reclaimed land. All subsequent development in the central area was 'floated' on expensive concrete rafts.

Grangemouth Stadium, Kersie Bank Avenue, 1966, Wilson & Wilson
Overlooking the greenery of Inchyra Park to the north, clean-lined design with metal Floclad superstructure over buff and dark brown brick. Features 7,000-spectator capacity and an all-weather running track, the first of its kind in Britain.

Inchyra Nursery School, Tinto Drive, 1982,
Central Regional Council Architectural Services
Attractive single-storey academy in variegated
pale red brick, dominated by central hall's slated
pyramid roof over deep timber fascia.

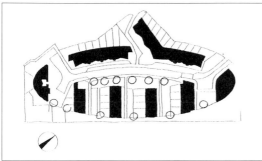

Top *Inchyra Nursery School.* Left and
above *Westerton Road housing.*

66 **Westerton Road housing**, 2001,
Page & Park Architects
Ingenious egg-shaped development of some
55 houses for Loretto Housing Association for
supported and mainstream tenants in
monopitch-roofed flatted blocks, west of the
open spaces of Inchyra Park (which doubles as a
clear blast zone between the housing and the
refinery). Focused around landscaped courtyards
and a central service spine road with parking off,
those blocks to the east, positioned with gable on
to the park. Tough blue bricks form the shell of
the egg, white and coloured renderings and
boarding the inside faces.

Wilson & Wilson evolved from an
amalgamation in 1938 of the Falkirk firms
of Strang & Wilson and Wilson & Tait.
Strang & Wilson was established in 1896.
In the 1930s, Alex Wilkie (later
Dumfriesshire burgh architect) and Alec
Currel (later Falkirk burgh architect) all
worked in the office. In 1940, the practice
opened a branch in Grangemouth, their
office in Falkirk from 1975 onwards being
at Arnot Grange, Maggie Wood's Loan.

67 **Church of the Holy Rood**, 1963, Wilson & Wilson
Pleasant 'cloister' comprising church, flat-roofed
hall and entrance ambulatory, the church having
steeply pitched and slated roof to its buttressed
A-frame structure. Simple cross and bell under
apex at fully glazed frontage, colourful stained
glass above the altar (see colour p.88).

Below *Church of the Holy Rood.*
Bottom *Folly, Inchyra Grange Hotel.*

Bowhouse Community Centre, 1965,
Wilson & Wilson
L-shaped group, hall having butterfly roof, a
popular architectural feature of those times, and
gridded timber fenestration.

Inchyra Grange Hotel
Scots Baronial with pedimented gables and
dormers, entered by way of porch in the angle.
Later additions to east and west including, to the
east, blind **gothic folly** and modern mansarded
and slate-clad block. In front, 1728 **sundial** on
modern plinth.

123

Central Scotland Airport.

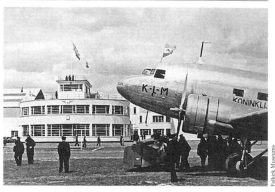

Falkirk Museums

Bothkennar Church
The Session met and after prayer Sederunt Minr. and Elders, Janet Findelson having acknowledged, that she was with Child to her Master Alexr. Lorn, Sailor at Newton and they being both cited to the Session, the Said Alexr. compeared and judicialy confessed that he was the father of the Child, that the said Janet Findelson was bigg with. Sic Subscribitur – Alexr. Lorn.
From the Session Minutes of 27 August, 1753

Below *Bothkennar Parish Church.*
Middle *Tombstone, Bothkennar churchyard, with beautifully carved ship and simply inscribed* James Sclanders and Ann Stewart, 1794. Bottom *Howkerse Farm.*

Central Scotland Airport, 1939, Alex Mair
Acting on the recommendations of the Maybury Report to build a central airport for Scotland, Scottish Aviation Ltd, with the characteristic fervour of the times, built on 600 acres near Inchyra Park a gleaming white semicircular terminal, complete with hangars in only three months. Its existence was short-lived, alas, all passenger services ceasing the same year with the outbreak of war. Officially closed June 1955 and demolished shortly after.

NORTH OF GRANGEMOUTH

Jaques

68 **Bothkennar Parish Church**, 1789, rebuild of earlier church, 1673? Remodelled and enlarged, 1887, Sydney Mitchell
Elegiacally sited, the old church's characterful four-stage tower with its slated ogival roof holding its own against Mitchell's large transept, belfry and porch additions.

Fine **tombstones** in *Great Expectations*-like **churchyard** include representations of ships, commemorating seamen of former ports of Airth and Carronshore. **Manse**, 1816, discreetly distant from church, in rubble with classical cornice at eaves and pilastered doorpiece. A good example of domestic dwelling of that period.

RCAHMS

Skinflats
Situated on the lands of Skinflats Farm, a cluster of more modern houses replaces those originally built for the miners of the Grangemouth Coal Company, 1845–1911.

Howkerse Farm, 1734
Two-storey farmhouse of some antiquity owned by the Crawford and Nimmo families since the 1730s; wing added early 19th century. Arched entrance to single-storey neighbour, pedestal **sundial** dated 1699 in garden.

Jaques

Tiendsyard

Dinky two-storey former post office with oversize central pedimented dormer. Possible tax-inspector's office. Tiends or taxes were exacted in the area by Polmont parish until 1928.

Newton

Only fragments remain of the late 17th-century mansion for the Bruces of Newton, including detached two-storey roofless ruin, possibly a servants' bothy.

SOUTH OF GRANGEMOUTH

Inveravon Tower, possibly 15th century
Ivy-clad ruin of tower, over 12ft in diameter, walls 5ft thick and vaulted chamber within. The *Auchinlech Chronicle* relates under March 1455: *James II kest down the Castell of Inverayne and sine incontinent passed till Glasgow* (at which time the castle belonged to the Hamiltons).

Top *Tiendsyard*. Above *Inveravon Tower*.

During an excavation at Inveravon, the oldest known skeleton of a dog in Britain was found, dating to between 5000 and 3000 BC. RCAHMS, *Stirlingshire*

Jinkabout Bridge

Worth a mention if only for its delightful name; where the river Avon takes one of its many bends and today the B904 crosses it.

69 **Avondale House**, *c*.1820,
(?)James Gillespie Graham
Symmetrical and brooding Gothick former Clarkstone, with battlements, pinnacled corner towers and advanced ecclesiastical centre bay on 16th-century site. In extensive grounds, it awaits restoration. Courtyard **stable block**, early 19th century, in similar vein integrated with entrance approach to the house.

Below *Avondale House*. Bottom *Folly*.

Folly, Avondale Park

On hill south west of house, castellated small square pavilion with circular towers at the angles looks like the real thing – from a distance! Must have fooled many a traveller on the motorway nearby. Now roofless ruin.

Polmont Woods

South of **Little Kerse Farm** lie Polmont Woods, location of **equestrian course**, **Milhall Reservoir**, **Grangemouth Golf Course** and **artificial ski-slope** at Polmonthill. It was at Polmonthill that the **Antonine Wall** crossed the River Avon as a bridge, the sites of Roman camps being discovered near the reservoir.

Kinneil Estate.

According to *Frier Mark Hamilton's Historie,* King Robert the Bruce gave all the lands of Kinneil to Sir Gilbert Hamilton, *for his trew service and great manheid* and especially for having slain *the great Lieutenant of Yngland upon Kynnale Muir.* From this same authority we learn, Sir Gilbert had been with Bruce in the field of Bannockburn, and was one of the seven knights that kept the king's person. For Sir Gilbert's exploits upon Kynnale Muir, King Robert *gaif till him his arms till weir in Scotland, three sinkfuilzes in ane bludy field.*

On moving the village, 1696, Lord John Hamilton writes to the Earl:
Daniel Hamilton is building you a fine park wall and remooving your little town (of Kinneil) *further from you, without your park wall, and building it a regular town. There are five or six houses almost built. He is likewise levelling your outer court and making a fine gravel walk throw the midle of it.*
I R Gow and A Rowan, *Scottish Country Houses*

KINNEIL AND BO'NESS

Bo'ness is to Kinneil as Grangemouth is to Bo'ness, each supplanting its predecessor as history unfolded. The differences were in the differing nature of the communities: Kinneil, feudal, its livelihood almost completely bound up with that of Kinneil House and its occupants; Bo'ness and Grangemouth both developed as first harbours, then trading posts on the Forth – Bo'ness in the days of sailing ships, Grangemouth in those of steam ships. The story of all three communities is that of 250 years of Scottish maritime history.

KINNEIL

The village predated Borrowstouness or Bo'ness by several hundred years. As the latter grew in the 17th century, so Kinneil declined, parish and church being officially suppressed in 1669.

70 **Kinneil Church,** 12th century
Only solitary western gable with double belfry remains of St Catherine's on its lofty perch, once a landmark for ships entering Bo'ness Harbour. Evidence of loft on south side, almost certainly the 'sailors loft' referred to in parish records of 1640 and 1646, just before church abandoned.

Above *Kinneil Church.* Right *Kinneil House.*

Kinneil House, from 16th century
Beginning as small tower extended into substantial one in 1540s and '50s by James

Hamilton, 2nd Earl of Arran and Governor of Scotland on lands given to his ancestors by Robert the Bruce. House comprises main **tower**, 1546–50, and **palace**, 1553. Partially destroyed, 1570, by the Earl of Morton, it was not until 1677, and as part of extensive alterations in the tower, possibly by James Smith, that Anne, Duchess of Hamilton added four-storey linking pavilions. Balancing south block intended but never carried out.

Palace of Kinneil was prominent throughout 16th century, being eastern seat of the Hamiltons, Earls of Arran and heirs to the throne. Monarchs frequently stayed here with the court. During demolition in 1936, Kinneil House was reprieved following discovery of 17th-century wall paintings in first-floor rooms of the palace. As a result the palace was taken into guardianship, as was the tower in 1975.

Tower, from 1546

Rubble shell five storeys high, three bays wide. Fenestration, small central doorway with arched pediment, massive cornice, balustrading and central ogival roof lantern all date from 1677. Surviving fireplaces suggest a great hall at first floor. Flanking it are two four-storey stairtowers and, on external wall of southern one, empty armorial frame which contained Hamilton arms and motto, now inside.

Unexecuted large addition by Sir Robert Lorimer, 1909, which included an internal court approached through a mansarded link block.

Kinneil House

From the early 18th century onwards the ducal family were infrequent residents at Kinneil and the house was let from time to time, two famous occupants being Dr John Roebuck of the Carron Iron Company, who lived there from 1760–94 and Dugald Stewart, the moral philosopher, resident in the early 1800s, and several of whose philosophical works were written at Kinneil.

In 1909 Sir Robert Lorimer proposed a huge redevelopment of Kinneil. None of his proposals was implemented.

Anne, Duchess of Hamilton, b.1636, the member of the family best known for her interest and involvement in the life of Kinneil and Borrowstoness. She was about 15 years of age when her Uncle William died without a male heir. In terms of the charter of Charles I to her father, Anne became Duchess of Hamilton in her own right. In 1656 she married William Douglas, a descendant of the Marquis of Douglas who was shortly afterwards granted the life title of Duke of Hamilton. Anne and William greatly enlarged Kinneil House. On this initiative, Kinneil and Borrowstouness were elected into a burgh of regality by royal charter in 1668 and the burgh was granted the privilege of a free port and harbour, which played a considerable part in laying the foundations on which the prosperity of Bo'ness was very quickly built.

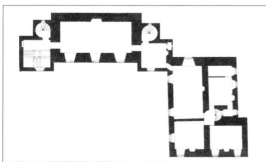

Plan of Tower and Palace by MacGibbon and Ross.

Tower doorway.

Palace, 1553
Long three-storey L-shaped wing, now partially roofed and served by single turnpike stair, terminates in two crowstepped gables, basements vaulted. On first floor, are twin jewels in Kinneil's crown the **Parable** and **Arbour Rooms**, former with illustrative murals, including 'The Good Samaritan', under panelled ceiling, and latter decorated with all manner of foliage, birds and beasts, roundels partially overlaid with simulated dado-height panelling, all under barrel-vaulting (see colour p.88). Also within palace, massive and very unusual 11th-century **cross** and **gravestones**. *Historic Scotland*

Today Kinneil looms up like a theatrical backdrop at the end of its long straight drive, foursquare to the east but perched precariously on precipitous side of the Gil Burn with its ivy-wrapped trees to the west, three menacing gunports being visible evidence of the defences that were needed to protect that approach. Also to be enjoyed are pleasant walks in **Kinneil estate** and **Deanburn Walkway**.

Partners and patent-holders in a project to develop an improved type of steam engine, James Watt and Dr John Roebuck hoped to use one to improve the pumping of water from the Bo'ness coal pits. Unsuccessful at first, Watt later teamed up with Matthew Boulton in Birmingham, their engines revolutionising the use of steam power in Britain's mills and factories.

Below *James Watt Cottage*.
Bottom *Kinneil Cottages*.

James Watt Cottage, 1768
Roofless ruin of minuscule stone cottage, near south gable of tower, erected as workshop for inventor James Watt.

At the end of the tree-lined drive, 17th-century gateposts, squared rubble with ashlar dressings, mark the entry to the original inner courtyard; to the south, a large **walled garden**, now put to fruitful use by the council.

Kinneil Cottages, 18th century
Rubble, crowstepped gabled, slated farm buildings and cottages, restored, 1974, by William A Cadell Architects. Saltire Society Award winner, 1974. All part of the footprint to the original outer entrance court to Kinneil House planned by Duchess Anne and comprising Duchess Anne Cottages, a handsome 18th-century group of estate buildings and cottages, the dormered stable building converted to Kinneil Museum. To the south an immaculate seven-bay terrace of late 18th-century cottages, all in rubble with crowstepping and pantiled roofs.

Kinneil Roman Fortlet, 142 AD
Situated west of the house and once part of the Antonine Wall, the northern frontier of the Roman Empire, it was built in the reign of Antoninus Pius to house some 20 soldiers and was defended by a

perimeter wall of turf blocks laid on a stone base. Finds from the fort excavations can be seen at Kinneil Museum.

Kinneil Colliery, 1964, Egon Riss
(demolished 1990s)
Major reconstruction of existing colliery, linking it and Valleyfield Colliery, Fife, by 3.4-mile tunnel under the Forth. Design typical of Riss's exciting combination of rigorously functional planning complemented by excitingly modern sculptural shapes in reinforced concrete, inspired by Le Corbusier's work – witness the two huge flared ventilator extracts. Closed 1983.

UPPER KINNEIL

To the west, at Nether Kinneil, the road passes under the railway bridge and climbs precipitously through the woods to the 100-ft contour and Upper Kinneil. From there it rollercoasts westwards providing sensational views over the Carse of Kinneil, now a bird sanctuary, and the Firth of Forth with the Cleish Hills of Fife beyond.

Profiting by the view and the location are **Upper Kinneil Farm**, a traditional single-storey courtyard group, and **Nether Kinneil Cottage**, 1985, John Cunningham, ingenious reconstruction of a double cottage with outshoots added on the diagonals including circular pavilion with conical roof and weathervane.

71 **Birkhill Clay Mine**
Developed by Mark Hurll in 1911 to provide clay for his Glenboig Brickworks, in beautiful location in the Avon Gorge south of Kinneil. Re-opened as tourist attraction by Bo'ness Heritage Trust in 1989. The charming bracketed and bargeboarded **station**, relocated from Monifieth in Angus by way of the 1988 Glasgow Garden Festival is now served by steam train from Bo'ness.

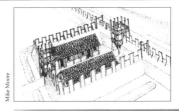

Top *Kinneil Roman Fortlet*. Above *Kinneil Colliery*.

Egon Riss, 1902-64, pioneering colliery architect, was educated in Vienna before studying at the Bauhaus, where he numbered among his friends, Kokoschka, Klee and Mahler. In Vienna he designed public buildings and houses of advanced design as well as producing a successful plan for Vienna city centre.

In 1938, to escape the Nazis, he came to Britain, served in the army and later taught briefly at the Architectural Association. On coming to Scotland, he built up a huge reputation in his chosen field of colliery design. Killoch in Ayrshire, Bilston Glen and Monktonhall in the Lothians, Seafield in Fife, as well as Kinneil all combined strict functional planning, usuallylinear, with great aesthetic awareness, particularly in his use of reinforced concrete undoubtedly inspired by the work of Le Corbusier but exhibiting great elegance.

A man of great charm and wide culture, Egon Riss is among those largely unsung heroes of modern architecture in Scotland.

Below *Nether Kinneil Cottage*. Left *Birkhill station*.

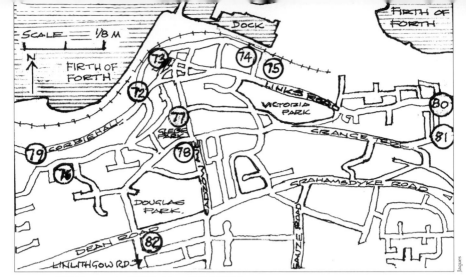

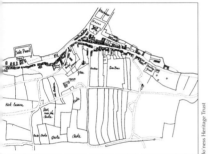

Above *Bo'ness, 1766.* Right *Bo'ness Harbour c.1890s.*

BO'NESS

Bo'ness, formerly Borrowstouness, began as a small fishing village on the promontory (or ness) around which the new town was to grow and prosper. Long established as a producer of coal and salt, its development as a port in the late 16th and 17th centuries was initiated by the powerful Hamilton family of nearby Kinneil Estate, whose village it was quickly to supersede. It was granted burgh status in 1668, and had its own Custom House by 1707. By the end of the 18th century, Bo'ness ranked as the third most important port in Scotland, eventually rivalling and then overtaking Blackness. However, the opening of the Forth and Clyde Canal in 1792 with its termination at Grangemouth put paid to Bo'ness' ambitions as Glasgow's east-coast port.

Bo'ness is on record as being a port as early as 1565. Between 1750 and 1780, it was one of the most thriving ports on the east coast. Much of the trade in the 17th and 18th centuries was with Holland and the Baltic countries. Coal and salt were the principal exports, grain, timber and flax being the main imports.

The construction of the first harbour was authorised by the Act of Parliament in 1707, but the present layout, with harbour protected by West Pier and an adjoining wet dock to the east, extended through lock gates dates from the reorganisation of 1881.

In 1705 Daniel Defoe wrote in the diary of his travels around Britain that: *the Bo'ness Sailors were the best seamen in the Firth and are very good pilots for the coast of Holland and the Baltic and the Coast of Norway.*

The town falls into three parts: the characterful, Baltic core of the old town, at one time clustered around the old harbour (now unfortunately, because of land reclamation, remote from it); looked down on from the heights behind by Victorian villas and an ecumenical rash of churches; and behind that, ever-expanding modern housing developments. The charm of Bo'ness, apart from the cosy intimacy of its centre with its palpable sense of history, lies in its precipitous slopes down which roads and braes twist and turn amid villas and abundant trees, giving rise to stunning prospects of the firth and beyond and affording astonishing and surprising views at every turn.

Architecturally, Bo'ness has benefited enormously from the work and strong personalities of two local heroes, Matthew Steele and James Thomson. The town has improved by leaps and bounds in the last decade, in the centre, the heritage area and in the huge improvements to the foreshore with its fine walks and regenerated dock basins. The challenge today is to bring back 24-hour life into the centre of what is only too often a ghost town. This would complement the superb advantages which the town already enjoys.

Matthew Steele, 1887–1937
A native of Bo'ness, Matthew Steele did his professional training in a Glasgow office before setting up on his own account in Bo'ness. He was architect for many buildings in the town and after the war carried out many important housing schemes for Bo'ness Town Council and West Lothian County Council. Unfortunately, many of his works have suffered terribly from neglect and vandalism including the Hippodrome in the centre of the town but there are signs that this neglect is now being rectified. In addition to the Hippodrome, his most interesting buildings are undoubtedly the Masonic Hall (at one time his office), the Bo'ness Iron Co. Building, Grangewells and his extensive housing in West Bo'ness. Influenced by Art Nouveau, no doubt following his years in Glasgow, he later graduated to a more Art Deco style in his later housing schemes but in all he touched he showed flair, wit and originality. His son, Alexander 'Sandy' Steele, became City Architect of Edinburgh.

Several years ago Mr Steele was joint sponsor for a proposed scheme for the formation of a huge dam across the Forth at South Queensferry to transform the upper reaches of the river and firth into an inland shipping lake, and to provide a road crossing between South and North Queensferry (from an obituary, 1937). Once a visionary, always a visionary!

Left *North Street.*

Town Centre
The old town grew up around the densely knit triangle formed by North and South Streets and the very narrow Scotland's Close (see p.4), which still retains much of its 18th-century character. **Waggon Road**, to the north, follows the route taken by the coal wagons from pits on the high ground to the harbour, and was constructed by the trustees of Dr John Roebuck in 1772; although still there, these routes now virtually eclipsed by the broad sweep of Union Street as it bypasses the town centre to the north severing the centre from the harbour and dock areas and costing Bo'ness much of its former maritime character.

Above *MacGibbon and Ross in the 1890s describe this attractive house in Scotland's Close with an ogival-roofed stairtower:* on the north side of the main street and towards its east end - with long row of dormers to the street and entered from a courtyard behind. *They add:* The Firth is now at a undesirable distance from this house but within living memory the tide rose and fell at the back of the courtyard. *Thought to have been the Duke of Hamilton's Town House, no trace remains.*

72 North Street
The Granary, Waggon Road, early 19th century Impressive five-storey stone warehouse, a legacy from the days when Bo'ness was a major exporter of grain, where North Street narrows and gives a seductive wiggle; restored, 1978, Falkirk District

Council Architects, now flats. With semicircular stairtower and hipped slate roof, its rows of wallhead chimneys (for drying the grain) give it an impressive castellated appearance. Saltire Society Award for Housing Area Rehabilitation Award 1980.

No 27, 19th century
Elegant pilastered frontage with rosette frieze to North Street and classical doorpiece to Waggon Road; restored, 1978, Falkirk District Council Architects. **Nos 21-25** Waggon Road, late 18th century, two storey and attic, two bay, harled, and **Nos 25-29** North Street, mid-19th century, overly fussy use of 'planners' stonework and roughcast fatally flaws what would otherwise be a brave attempt to provide a symmetrically planned streetscape with dormers in crisp pantile roofs. Restored, 1980, Falkirk District Council Architects.

Top *The Granary*. Above *27 North Street.* Right *'Tobacco' Warehouse.*

Tobacco Trade
Most of the North American tobacco shipped into the Clyde in the later part of the 18th century was exported to France as raw leaf, by way of selected east coast ports.

73 **'Tobacco' Warehouse**, Scotland's Close, 1772
Four-storey stone block with squared margins and quoins, square pyramid-roofed tower to rear, presents powerful fenestrated gable to Waggon Road and the sea, its attic lit by a lonely oculus. Keystone to arched entrance inscribed *IC 1772*. The building was a tobacco warehouse, the numerous fireplaces used for controlling the humidity of the leaf.

Old West Pier Tavern, Scotland's Close, from 1711
Two storey, four bay, with pilastered doorway in homely gable, stone and timber forestair in the close; lintel over door inscribed *17FMG MR11*. Some panelling on first floor with chimneypiece and ceiling plasterwork in front room. A welcoming sight to those just off the boats.

Old West Pier Tavern.

Bo'ness Library, Scotland's Close, 1978,
Falkirk District Council Architects
Conversion making good use of the ground
floors of the 18th-century 'tobacco' warehouse
and the Old West Pier Tavern linking both with a
two-storey stone block with curved corner (best
appreciated from outside), semicircular
stairtower and deep slated entrance fascia.

Harbour, Union Street, from 1707
Harbour improved, 1842, but, with its basin,
underwent major reorganisation in 1881 when
dock opened. Part of east pier dates from 1773,
with additions, 1787. Now separated from town
by the railway line, it was originally reached
directly by narrow streets such as Scotland's Close.

Dymock's Buildings, 47-51 North Street,
late 17th/early 18th century
Bo'ness' oldest house, and incorporating 1650
merchant's house. Much altered two-and-a-half
storeys, white painted with black window
surrounds and corrugated-iron roof. Courtyard to
north with high stone wall. Wooden panelling
and fireplaces survive on the first floor. Such a
fine visual stop to the west end of North Street.
Under restoration proposals by the National
Trust for Scotland.

Anchor Tavern, 44-46 North Street, 1891, Andrew
Colville
Two-and-a-half storey, with appropriate fish-scale
slated roof to corbelled corner tower picks up
baronial theme opposite.

Hippodrome, Hope Street, 1911, Matthew Steele
Masterpiece by this inspired son of Bo'ness, for
Louis Dickson, comprising circular auditorium
with shallow domed roof, twin entrances and
wedge-shaped stage block. John Taylor's 1926
addition at the vennel corner, with its own mini-
dome, though competent, spoils the symmetry of
the original façade.
  The future of Steele's 'Picture Palace' is the
future of Bo'ness centre, as its strong circular
form, acts as a natural pivot for North Street and

Bo'ness Library.

***Passed thro' Borrowstoness**, a town on
the Firth, inveloped in smoke from the great
salt pans and vast collieries near it. The
town house is built in the form of a castle.
There is a good quay, much frequented by
shipping, for considerable quantities of coal
are sent from hence to London and there are
besides some Greenland ships belonging to
the town.*
Thomas Pennant, *A Tour in Scotland*, 1769

Below *Dymock's Buildings.*
Left *Hippodrome*. Bottom *Ground-floor
plan by Matthew Steele.*

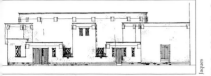

could, with an imaginative development of shops and cafés and good landscaping, become the focus for a town centre second to none in Scotland. Sadly derelict, its future is under active consideration by many bodies including the Scottish Historic Buildings Trust.

Town Clock and Lamps, Market Square, 1984
Cast iron, with sporting dolphins on its base, gifted by Ballantine's Foundry and based on design of decorative lamp standards supplied to Middle East Oil States. Also throughout the town, 19th-century cast-iron lamp **standards** each stamped Falkirk Iron Co., Falkirk NB (for North Britain).

Post Office, East Pier Street, 1911, James Thomson
Solid four-square affair, with piended roof, shallow projecting bays and channelled ground-floor stonework, chunky keystones to its first floor windows set in deep banded cornice. *The Post Office* is writ large in similar cornice at eaves level between massive chimneystacks.

Top *Hippodrome, Hope Street elevation by Matthew Steele*. Middle *Town Clock and Lamps*. Above *Post Office*.

Below *74 North Street*. Bottom *South Street*.

Clydesdale Bank, *c*.1900
Handily fronting onto Market Square, smart red sandstone block with chunky squared stone surrounds to entrance and ground-floor windows.

Jubilee Drinking Fountain, 1887
Erected on site of old Cross Well, also known as St John's Well and one of the original main water supplies for the town. Granite-based with spray of ornamental lamps over, gifted by James Allan on occasion of Queen Victoria's Golden Jubilee.

74 North Street, 1786, restored, 1983, William A Cadell
Very handsome three storeys with attic, façades enlivened with stone bandings at floor levels, windows and corners. Note traditional scrolled skewputts, the keystoned architrave to entrance and wallhead chimneystacks on all sides.

South Street
Starts at the fork near The Granary, hugs the contours at the foot of the brae, then narrows to a very cosy width at the east end junction with North Street. Traces of the old town plan remain in Gibson's Wynd and the steep lanes which climb up towards the 100ft contour and from which outstanding views over the town and firth can be obtained.

Nos 9, 11 & 13, an interesting trio in their run through the styles of the centuries, all sensitively restored, 1981, by William A Cadell Architects for Falkirk District Council. **No 9**, early 19th century, Georgian, three storeys, three bays, with deep band course separating upper stonework from painted ground floor; circular stairtower to rear.

Left 9, 11 & 13 South Street. Above *11 South Street. In point of fact, Steele's magnificent shop front is part of the 1981 restorations. His client John Paris, having panicked at the sight of such an ambitious design had built only the upper two floors to Steele's plans.*

No 11, 1907, Matthew Steele
Harled, with ashlar dressings, second- and third-floor windows grouped to form dormer tower above dramatic semicircular shopfront. Superb details; delicate cornice at first floor, swept eaves soffit, splayed abutments of shopfront. One of Steele's best with not a little of the Mackintosh touch. Prima donna of the group given posthumous kiss of life, 1981, by William A Cadell Architects.

No 13, 1750 (see p.5)
Distinguished harled five-bay façade in best Scottish tradition, originally tolbooth, with continuous sill and lintel courses to first-floor windows. Door with inset panel over, giving date and initials *1750 RB/EB*. A 1647 date stone on the gable of the present building may well be from earlier tolbooth on same site. Inside at first floor, some original panelling and chimneypieces; notable survival of original glazing bars.

No 25, Anderson Building, 1902, with central chimneystack, by James Thomson, as are, **Nos 54-58**, 1900, on axis of Market Street, elaborate five-bay block with decorative sill panels, Corinthian pilasters and pediment.

Sammy Baird's Bar, 1900
Former Turf Tavern at foot of School Brae with flamboyant broken pediment over splayed corner.

25 South Street.

John Anderson after whom the building is named, was the town's most prosperous banker, shipowner and merchant in the 1900s. Owning several of the town's whaling vessels as well as the whale-oil works he earned his title as the 'Uncrowned King of Bo'ness'.

Sammy Baird's Bar.

Salmon Court, 1977, Alison & Hutchison & Partners
In roughcast with slated roofs, well-planned retirement complex climbs the hill behind, its conservatory-type common room on top profiting by the views, entrance at ground level by way of three-storey block, set back from general street frontage.

First Edition, 1883
Scots Baronial corner block with datestone and ogee roof to its corner turret. **No 68**, Serafinis, late 18th century, finest block in street, its regular façade interrupted by raised and pilastered centre with split pediment framing arched attic window.

Journal and Gazette Building, North Street, 1887
Eyestopping Scots Baronial block on gusset site with slimline corner tower topped with splendidly macho candle-snuffer roof. Crisp astrological carvings embellish the window pediments on top. Restored, 1986, William A Cadell Architects.

West of East Pier Street, site of old **Town Hall**, 1780, foursquare with battlemented corner turrets and central four-stage clock tower. Tower, which later sported a perky pyramidal roof, survived the demolition of the hall, but was demolished in the 1960s owing to mining subsidence. The fine **Douglas Hotel**, which stood to the east, suffered the same fate.

Main Street
Shop, East Partings, 1911, Matthew Steele
Exactly right for its gusset site. Characterful cube with huge windows, splayed corners and chevron decoration, which would greatly benefit from a coat of paint.

Top 68 South Street. Middle Journal and Gazette Building. Above Old Town Hall.

Town Hall
Described in the *First Statistical Account* of 1796 as: *an exact model of Inveraray House, built at the head of the harbour, about twenty years ago by the Duke of Hamilton. The ground floor was intended for a Prison, the second for a Court Room and the attic storey for a School. But, the original intentions not having been carried into execution, this fine building is going into ruin.*

Shops and **houses**, 1932, Matthew Steele
Two first-class two- and three-storey roughcast blocks enliven the junction with Commissioner Street, both blocks splayed at the corners and incorporating jazzy link panels between

Shop, East Partings.

windows. Now, happily restored to their former glory. Note deep horizontal articulation in board-marked concrete frontage between houses and shops in the block to the west – Steele never missed an opportunity to provide visual interest and excitement.

Carrier's Quarters, 1904, James Thomson, and **Gardener's Arms**, late 19th century, probably James Thomson
Bargeboarded gabling, recessed bays below with transplanted 1671 date stone bearing initials *RSI*. Adjacent Gardener's Arms is stone, with shallow ball-finialed pediment; handsome pub front picked out in black and white.

Union Street, a generous sweep of ring road that links east and west of town centre to the north by side of harbour and wet dock.

Top *Shops and Houses, Main Street and Commissioner Street*. Above *Carrier's Quarters and Gardener's Arms*.

Bo'ness Police Station, Commissioner Street, 1981, Central Regional Council Architectural Services
Highly unfortunate dirge in concrete block trying to ape neighbouring Customs House, including projecting bays. At the rear, circular stairtowers with truncated conical roofs.

Customs House, Union Street, 1880, William Simpson
Narrow, two-storey, block overlooking the shore with shallow hip-roofed bays, linking stringcoursing, punchy gable windows and sprightly cast-iron roof finials.

74 **Bo'ness Iron Company**, Union Street, 1908, Matthew Steele
Heavily modelled two storeys, five unequal bays, with Art Nouveau details, in rubble with ashlar dressings, happily now cleaned up. One of Steele's most interesting buildings, undoubtedly inspired by Mackintosh's Glasgow School of Art, its first phase by then completed, even to the recessed bays, sporadic roof projections, asymmetrical north entrance frontage and details including the

Bo'ness Iron Company or the Dock Foundry was established in 1900, although ironfounding had started in Bo'ness in 1836 with the firm of Steele, Miller & Company, later the Bo'ness Foundry Company. The other well-known Bo'ness firm, Ballantine's New Grange Foundry was established in 1856 further east in Main Street. As well as standard cast-iron products such as kitchen ranges and manhole covers, speciality items produced by Bo'ness ironfounders ranged from ornate lamp standards for Arab princes to replacement cannon for Edinburgh Castle and in Victorian times, Bo'ness ironworkers were responsible for forging the barbed tips of the long harpoons on which ultimately the success of the whaling industry depended.

Left and below *Bo'ness Iron Company*.

Above *Doorway detail, Bo'ness Iron Company*. Right *Bo'ness Heritage Area*.

elaborate water hoppers (see *Central Glasgow* in this series). The major elements of the composition clamped between macho stone columns projecting well above roof level, the window mullions articulated with large cubist blocks in the classical manner and the angled bay at the corner with its build-up of castellated crown parapet and timbered gable above. Two cafes inside, one up, one down, the quality of their decor well-intended but best not discussed, the lotus flower newels of Steele's stair a victim of the new layout. Such a wealth of architectural invention for such a small building! A connoisseur's building if ever there was, to be cherished by Scotland and Bo'ness alike.

Bo'ness & Kinneil Railway
Since 1979, the Scottish Railway Preservation Society has been transforming a greenfield site beside the old dock basin into the nucleus of a living steam railway. New track has been laid connecting Bo'ness to Birkhill by way of Kinneil, the trip affording magnificent views of the foreshore and Forth. The line goes to Manuel, where it joins the main line.

The area of land around the old harbour and wet dock was once packed with a network of some seven miles of railway track and sidings. A rail link ran east to Carriden and west to Kinneil.

Below *Engine shed*. Bottom *Former Wormit Station*.

75 Bo'ness Heritage Area
On site beside old Dock Basin, former Haymarket (Edinburgh) **train shed**, 1840–2, John Miller, eight bays of former 12-bay shed re-erected here by Scottish Railway Preservation Society, 1979. Fluted cast-iron columns support elliptical arched arcade with decorative spandrels. Also **engine shed**, in variegated brickwork, bargeboarded **station** from Wormit, Fife, and **Hamilton's Cottages**, typical railway workers' dwellings. A **light railway** operates between Bo'ness and Birkhill Clay Mine via Kinneil. Stupendous views across the Forth best obtained from the cast-iron footbridge that crosses the railway at the west of the site.
Guide and timetable available

Upper Bo'ness
Victorian Bo'ness very wisely hitched up her skirts and retreated from the noise and congestion of the old town up Providence Brae and School Brae (see p.3). It established layered levels of respectability with a sprinkling of fine churches to the west along Stewart Avenue and Braehead and to the east along Grange Terrace. The latter enjoys sensational views through the trees over Victoria Park to the estuary and the hills of Fife beyond (see colour p.88). Street names are redolent of former sea-faring times:

Providence Brae, at one time a haven from the pressgangs; Tidings Hill, a look-out for the returning whaler.

76 **Bo'ness Old Parish Church**, Panbrae Road, 1885, Shiells & Thomson
Gaunt and magisterial, gothic, squared rubble with ashlar dressings, built to replace original parish church in Corbiehall and a landmark for miles around. Impressively aisled and cruciform in plan, with stepped transepts giving access to three lofts (for lairds, mariners and miners); main entrance in base of lofty four-stage tower with flèche spire. Within, **stained glass** includes work by William Meikle & Sons, 1902 and William Wilson, 1938, a **memorial** by J Blyth, 1949, to James Thomson, architect and over the door to the laird's loft, the **coat of arms** of the Duke of Hamilton who subscribed to the cost of the building. To the rear, **church hall**, 1911, Matthew Steele. Six-bay extension in the style of the church, neatly articulated at its west end by an advanced and pedimented mini-bay.

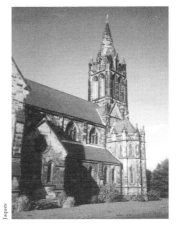

Bo'ness Old Parish Church.

James Thomson, d.1949
Well known Bo'ness architect whose distinctive style, often incorporating the rhythms of bargeboarded gables, helped to enrich the streetscapes of his native town. Key buildings include the Post Office, Anderson Building, Carrier's Quarters, the Crown Inn, Grangepans (see pp.134, 135, 137 & 145).

Riverview Hotel, Church Wynd, early 19th century
Single-storey ashlar villa with dormers, pilastered and pedimented doorpiece; 1876 extension to rear has dormer with broken pediment and stone eagle up top; tripartite window to dormer supported on scrolled brackets.

Left and below Town Hall and Carnegie Library.

77 **Town Hall** and **Carnegie Library**, Stewart Avenue, 1901–4, George Washington Browne
Large and elegant classical structure dominating the town, with a nautical look in the way it rides the contours like a great ship at the foot of **Glebe Park**. Beautifully detailed ashlar stonework, hall to west, library to east. Distinctive features are its noble apsidal west end, projecting semicircular bays, large semicircular thermal windows at first floor, octagonal lantern and two clock towers on its piended slate roof (similar to those at Robert Adam's Register House, see *Edinburgh* in this series). Clocks by H and R Millar.

The building was a gift to the town from Scotland's most famous benefactor, the steel magnate Andrew Carnegie. Today, the library service has moved to Scotland's Close but hall well used for public functions.

Victorian Bandstand, Glebe Park, 1902 Walter McFarlane and Co. Saracen Foundry, Glasgow, cast-iron, octagonal, with slated roof, brackets and lacy crown cupola of incredible delicacy.

War Memorial, Stewart Avenue On site with panoramic view of Forth estuary, elegant granite cenotaph to dead of First World War.

78 **Craigmailen UF Church**, Braehead, 1883, McKissack & Rowan Early English in style, having lofty buttressed tower with crown spire at north-west corner and entered by door in north gable under pointed arch carved with vines. Within galleries on three sides under a ceiling painted with flowers and stars.

Top *Victorian Bandstand.* Above *Craigmailen UF Church.* Right *Bo'ness Public School.*

Porch, St Catherine's Episcopal Church.

Bo'ness Public School, School Brae, 1875, John Paterson Two well-articulated and finely crafted Victorian classical blocks, former Anderson Academy, on a sloping site with bullseye window in the central pediment of the east one. Clean-limbed modern **link block**, 1987, Central Regional Council Architectural Services, with asymmetrical slated roof and galleried hall in concrete block within.

St Catherine's Episcopal Church, Cadzow Crescent, 1921, Dick Peddie & Walker Todd Minute and utterly charming Norman style church in rubble with sanctuary, chancel, crossing and transepts entered through beautifully detailed and heavily buttressed porch under arched doorway with packed slate voussoirs.

Tidings Hill, Cadzow Crescent, 1908,
A Hunter Crawford
Dominating this part of the town, large roughcast
and stone-trimmed L-plan mansion of two and
three storeys, in extensive sloping grounds,
signalled by huge triple-stacked chimney on
north-west face. Within, ground-floor plan
developed round 40ft oak-panelled hall with
inglenook. Shallow curved bays to dining and
morning rooms; magnificent Victorian
conservatory with apsidal end.

Flats, Cadzow Crescent, 1935, Matthew Steele
Interesting group of four flat-roofed semidetached
two-storey blocks for Bo'ness Town Council,
entrances at the gables for sociability, angled corner
windows for views. Harled, with Art Deco concrete
'streamlining' between windows. Now with
inappropriately heavy, shallow-pitch tile roofs.
Similar block in Stewart Avenue (see colour p. 88).

Top *Tidings Hill drawn by A Hunter
Crawford*. Above *Flats, Cadzow Crescent.*

Alexander Hunter Crawford, 1865–1945,
served his apprenticeship in London and
worked with London County Council.
Returning to Edinburgh in 1890, he
practiced with Rowand Anderson and
Frank Worthington Simon from
1899–1902. Apart from Edinburgh's
Masonic Hall, he mostly designed grand
houses until he became chairman of the
family biscuit-making business.

Left *Masonic Hall*. Below *131-135
Stewart Avenue.*

Stewart Avenue
Masonic Hall, 1908, Matthew Steele
Truly marvellous little edifice for 408 Lodge
Douglas, at one time Steele's own office, which by
virtue of a few subtle and unusual details raises the
building to the realms of musical composition. Its
main themes, a steeply pitched, hipped roof, a
massive Aztec-style and pedimented entrance
porch with Masonic emblems, both supported on
stumpy tapered columns, and a recessed loggia
give this diminutive work an epic architectural
scale and richness. Within, a barrel-vaulted hall at
the lower level.

Nos 131-135, 1909, Matthew Steele
Imaginative asymmetrical, semidetached flats for
John Burnet. In 'spotted dick' rubble, its
variously hipped and gabled frontages, huge
shed roof to west, single- and double-storey bays,
all form part of architect's sophisticated game
with the most basic of architectural components.

Matthew Steele was an architect who,
within the functional demands of his
brief, continued experimenting both
formally and stylistically – here at 131-
135 Stewart Avenue would seem, in the
rugged mode of American architect H H
Richardson (1838–86). The latter's work,
which included both large public
buildings and smaller private
residences, would almost certainly have
been known by Steele and was
distinguished by a certain ruggedness
allied to formal inventiveness. His best-
known work was his Marshall Field
Wholesale Store in Chicago of 1885.

The Knowe.

Ochil Tower, Stewart Avenue, 1930s/40s
Painted and balustraded villa with castellated
corner tower provides suitable seaside flavour
while advertising its view.

The Knowe, Erngath Road, 1879, A Porteous
Unremarkable two- and three-storey Victorian
double-plan villa, for George Cadell Stewart, on
steeply sloping site, extended, 1907, by Matthew
Steele with domed and classically cosseted rooftop
eyrie astride existing baronial booster rocket
tower, and again in 1912 with wildly cantilevered
billiard room at third-floor level. Total effect is
staggering, as of some curious tree-house.

Grange Terrace
Boasts many fine sandstone villas lining the
south side of the street overlooking Victoria Park,
the town and river. Built by 19th-century
merchants, ship owners and industrialists, to a
strict feuing plan, they now rightfully form part
of the town's Victorian conservation area.

St Andrew's Parish Church, 1905, J N Scott and
A Lorne Campbell
Cruciform plan, finely crafted, with convincing
blend of perpendicular and Art Nouveau details,
entered in buttressed corner tower, having
battlemented parapet, slim copper spire and
octagonal stair turretlet with tasselled toorie top.
Within, boarded roof with triple king-post **gallery**
and some fine **stained glass**, one, 'St Andrew and
St Michael', 1920, by Oscar Paterson.

*St Andrew's Parish Church drawn by
J N Scott and A Lorne Campbell.*

Opposite from top *Walden; Caer Edin;
Old Grange House, 1564 (demolished
1906), corbelled corner turret preserved
and built into The Grange, Linlithgow
(see* **West Lothian** *in this series); Station
Hotel; Former Bo'ness Old Kirk.*

Walden, 6 Grahamsdyke Avenue, 1906,
Matthew Steele
Two-storey harled L-plan villa with square bay
window to east gable, Art Nouveau tapered
chimneys and small timbered inset porch in the
angle. As at Grangewells in Muirhouses (see
p.154) Steele's hand is more readily discernible in
the small details such as tapered chimneystacks
and flared copes, the treatment of the gable apex
and the louvred ventilators to the loft.

Caer Edin, Grahamsdyke Avenue, 1899,
(?)W G Rowan
Handsome Tudor-gabled stone villa for timber
importer Sir Richard Murray (now flats) with
Ionic doorpiece between bay windows. Within,
columned hallway, golden Baltic pine panelling,
plaster ceilings, stained glass and nautical free-
standing fireplace. Now converted to flats.
Byland, opposite, an imposing villa with arched
entrance and circular turret.

WEST PARTINGS
Station Hotel, 5-11 Seaview, 1936, Matthew Steele
Fascinating terraced Art Deco hotel, shops and
houses, comprising two-storey centre section with
three-storey end blocks, the latter with shallow
piended slate roofs (note there are no external
down pipes or gutters – instead a cheekily recessed
and banded eaves detail).

The frontage of the hotel (No 11), curves deftly
into the foot of Providence Brae, the bar entrance
signalled by a wafer-thin concrete circular canopy.
This, the original fenestration, hotel sign and other
felicitous details are now no more. Basics remain,
the smooth creamy stone gift-wrapped at eaves
and base with ink-green bandings.

Former Bo'ness Old Kirk, 1638
In use as Star Cinemas bingo hall and store.
Supplanted parish church of Kinneil, aisle added
by the Duke of Hamilton in 1672, subsequent
rebuildings in 1775 and 1820. **Cinema** frontage,
1915, Matthew Steele, exhibiting his confident
handling of masses is in popular Egyptian style.
The **graveyard**, containing many interesting late
17th- and 18th-century gravestones, is bisected by
Church Wynd.

Corbiehall
With the coal seams of Kinneil to the west and
saltpans in abundance to the east, this narrow strip
of land between the shoreline of the Forth and the
foot of the raised beach behind has been

43-51 Corbiehall.

The Sea Box Society was formed in 1634 by the masters of the port of Borrowstouness, for benevolent purposes and mutual help in times of need. The Society carried on for the next 100 years with great success in what was largely a sea-faring community. By the mid-17th century, the town contained a thriving community of brewers, maltsters and traders who combined in 1659 to form a Landsmen's Box. Subsequent dissent and secessions resulted in yet another grouping, the Shipmaster's Society. All three prospered for some time, but in later years with the building of the Forth & Clyde Canal, and the use of Grangemouth as a trading port, Bo'ness lost much of its trading prestige and in 1863 they amalgamated under the title of the United General Seabox, which still exists today.

Above 101 & 103 Corbiehall. Right St Mary's Building.

Corbiehall Graveyard, which was situated between road and foreshore on the middle of Corbiehall, was used for the burial of victims of the cholera epidemic of 1851. As a busy seaport, the town frequently experienced outbreaks of plague, cholera and other infectious diseases. This area in general has a macabre history. Not far from the graveyard was Bo'ness' place of execution. Here on 23 December 1679, after imprisonment in the town's tolbooth, five local witches and their warlock were burnt at the stake for 'consorting with the devil'.

continually populated since the early 1770s. Today, with the industries gone and the foreshore cleaned of dereliction, there are bracing walks to be had with marvellous views across the Forth to the north and wooded hills behind to the south.

43-51 Corbiehall, 1935, Matthew Steele
Known locally as 'Coffin Square' because of huge coffin-shaped doorway features to the individual blocks. A good example of Steele's readiness to make use of the simplest elements as interesting shapes for his urban form-making.

71-83 Corbiehall, 1905
Tenement with balustraded semicircular corner inscribed *Thomson Place* and **plaque** commemorating the establishment of the Bo'ness Sea Box Society in 1634.

101 & 103 Corbiehall, late 18th century
In rubble and pantiles with original forestair to upper floor. The last survivor of several such cottages in the 'Dardanelles', as these buildings were known.

79 **St Mary's Building**, Corbiehall, 1932, Matthew Steele
Against wooded backdrop of the raised beach above, boldly conceived and extensive three-storey terraced block, its horizontals echoing those of the foreshore and estuary to the north, articulated by five huge doorway features in the 'Egyptian cinema style', the end ones pedimented. An early and brave attempt at a 20th-century urbanism comparable to, but a good deal less bombastic than, say, the work of Ricardo Bofill in France. Scotland's towns, large and small, could still learn much from Steele.

Gilburn Cottage, 5 Grangemouth Road, 1907,
Matthew Steele
Providing a suitably light-hearted grace-note at
the west end of the town, tiny buttressed and
gabled cottage with all the marks of this always
interesting architect, including here the delightful
little slated coolie hats that cap the buttresses.

Snab Brae Redevelopment, Wotherspoon
Avenue, 1970, Scott & McIntosh
On former mining ground, 100 single- and two-
storey houses, pleasantly articulated and
linked, with tiled monopitch roofs and painted
window surrounds. **SSHA Housing**,
conventional and split-roof, two-storey houses
climbing the contours.

Top *Gilburn Cottage*. Above *Snab Brae
Redevelopment*.

EAST BO'NESS
Grangepans, Bridgeness and Carriden were all at
one time separate villages dotted along the
foreshore. Grangepans was incorporated into
Bo'ness in 1894 *much to the disgust of the whole
inhabitants!* Today they are linked together by
their various industries, including the timber
mills along the coastal strip and to the south by
their respective housing areas. It is to be hoped
that the presently neglected foreshore at
Carriden will be developed as well as has that to
the west.

GRANGEPANS
Takes its name from one of the town's earliest
industries and refers to the saltpans belonging to
the Grange estate. In post-medieval times there
were 13 saltpans in production, finally ceasing in
1890s.

Below *The Crown*. Bottom *16-24
Craigfoot Terrace*.

Grangepans Housing, 1968–9, Alison & Hutchison
& Partners, coherent layout of two-storey houses,
varied by four-storey flats over shops.

The Crown, 1908, James Thomson
Triple bargeboarded gables, front articulated by
large rainwater hoppers and downpipes.
Recessed bay windows below, all as in the
Carrier's Quarters, also by Thomson (see p.137).

80 **16-24 Craigfoot Terrace**, Cowdenhill, 1890,
James Thomson
Impressive half-timbered terrace for Henry
Cadell in stone and slates with large central
dormer flanked by four bargeboarded gables.
Thomson always enjoys the rhythms obtained by
the use of these simple features.

Top *Coronation Cottages.*
Above *Gladstone Terrace.*

Bo'ness Potteries
Brainchild of the indefatigable Dr John Roebuck, co-founder of Carron Iron Company, Bo'ness Pottery began production around 1766, using imported clay from Devon to produce the distinctive opaque porcelain ware, Bosphorous and Willow, much of it decorated with transfer patterns, and the ever-popular 'wally dugs', brightly painted cockerels and wedding mugs.

C W McNay established Bridgeness Pottery in 1886 which remained in operation until the 1950s. During the 20th century, the type of pottery produced changed from the transfer-printed tableware of the earlier periods and became much plainer, sold largely in Ireland or to Woolworth's and hospital contracts.

Bridgeness Tower and housing.

81 Philpingstone Road

Laid out by H M Cadell in 1897, intended as the beginning of a model *garden suburb* to the east of the town to house his miners and other workers. It focuses on Bridgeness Tower to its east.

Coronation Cottages, 1902, G Wightman
Attractive and well proportioned gabled and dormered terrace in cheerful red reconstituted blaes block with Gothick frieze at eaves level. Inscribed plaque *HMC 1902.*

Gladstone Terrace, 1905
Flamboyant crowstepped wallhead chimneys, variously pedimented doorways and huge scrolled skewputts.

51-75 Philpingstone Terrace, 1905, J M Dick Peddie (demolished)
Excellent two-storey-and-attic harled terraced cottages with baroque pediments, bullseye windows and dormers.

BRIDGENESS

Bridgeness pier first appears on a map of 1775, its small harbour used by vessels employed in the coal trade. At a later date Bridgeness became a centre for ship breaking, its yard one of the first in Scotland to tackle iron hulls before the days of oxyacetylene cutters. **Bridgeness Pottery**, another of its industries, was founded in 1886 and operated until the 1950s.

Bridgeness Tower, Harbour Road, 1750
Eyecatching circular tower with attached turretlet, harled with brick parapets. Reconstructed former windmill, for David Stevenson, shipmaster, and wife, used as observatory. Thereafter a very chequered career; Hippolyte Blanc added battlemented top storey as part of flat conversion for H M Cadell of Grange, 1895, and conversion by W A Cadell Architects, 1988, uses the tower as focus for group of two-storey houses. Saltire Society Award Commendation 1990.

Bridgeness Distance Slab, *c.*142 AD, Antonine Wall
Set into stone wall on west side of Harbour Road,
replica of inscription on 9ft-long ornately carved
Roman slab unearthed nearby in 1868. The splendid
original is now in the Museum of Scotland.

Doocot, Kinningars Park, (?)late 17th/early 18th
century
To the east of this beautiful tree-surrounded and
sloping park, lectern doocot, lower part altered,
18th century, to form winding house, whose
capped and enclosed shaft is nearby; a reminder of
the numerous coal and ironstone mines in this
area. Upper part has 415 brick nesting boxes.

New Grange House, from 1857
Extensive, much-altered property in stone and
roughcast, the original L-plan house overlaid with
Victorian and later additions and entered under
crowstepped gable. Until the building of The
Grange on Airngarth Hill above Linlithgow Loch
in 1908 (see *West Lothian* in this series), this was the
residence of the Cadells of Grange, following the
move from the original and much finer house at
what is now the school site at Grange Loan.

Bridgeness Cottage, late 18th century
Fine harled and slated house, circular stairturret to
rear, painted margins to door and windows.

Grange Schoolhouse, 1906, James Thomson
Triple-gabled stone villa, its two-bay windows
cleverly integrated with continuous porch under
single monopitch roof.

Victoria Saw Mills, 1922–4, Matthew Steele
Hipped and slated office block with characterful
and beautifully detailed off-centre pedimented
entrance feature comprising doorway and flanking
windows the large lintel over inscribed *Victoria Saw
Mills*. Adjacent blood-red ply-clad shed of unusual
cranked section with distinctly Baltic flavour.

Cuffabouts or Causewayfoot
A part of East Bo'ness worth a mention if only for
its interesting name. Causeways were for the
conveyance of coal by 'creels' on horseback to the
boats waiting at anchor, *c.*1880.

The **Bridgeness Distance Slab** (*left*) is
only one of a number of stone tablets
that the Roman soldiers set into the
superstructure of the Antonine Wall to
commemorate the construction work
completed by particular units (much
like our 'topping out' ceremonies). The
tablet may originally have marked the
eastern end of the wall which ran along
the lines of Dean Road and
Grahamsdyke Road. Flanking the
central inscription are two sculptural
panels, one depicting a cavalryman
riding down native tribesmen, the other
an animal sacrifice. The inscription, in
translation, reads: *In honour of the
Emperor Caesar Titus Aelius Hadrianus
Antoninus Augustus Pius, Father of his
Country, The Second Legion, Augustus'
own, executed the work for 4652 paces.*

Doocot, Kinningars Park.

Below *Bridgeness Cottage*. Middle
Grange Schoolhouse. Bottom *Victoria
Saw Mills*.

Above *47-49 Dean Road, 1905, Matthew Steele, his first commission.*

Below *St Mary's of the Assumption RC Church.* Middle and bottom *Seaforth.*

Dean Road/Grahamsdyke Road/Gauze Road
Victorian and modern villas, many of excellent quality, fight it out for a place in the sun at the top of the hill overlooking the town; **Kinglass Park**, a triangle of greenery with ship's mast flagpole as centrepiece.

To the north, a variety of roads, such as Erngath Road and Grahamsdyke Avenue, scamper down the slope, some directly, some crab-wise, to the old town.

Bo'ness Hospital, 1910 (demolished 1999)
Built as a fever hospital with verandas and balconies, now used for geriatric and outpatient accommodation; on sloping site, symmetrical white-rendered single-storey group with Tudor gables and appropriately overbearing two-storey matron's block.

Health Centre, 1981, Alison & Hutchison & Partners
Not very therapeutic flat-roofed red brick box with black-stained timber plant-room housing on roof.

Kinneil Primary School, Dean Road
Irregular group in stone and roughcast with shallow pitched copper roof. Pillars to porch support wafer-thin slab roof.

St Mary of the Assumption RC Church, 1960, Gillespie, Kidd & Coia (demolished 1988)
Act of religious vandalism has resulted in the loss of one of the most interesting early churches of this talented firm. Flat-roofed, white-rendered concertina of splayed walls, widening towards the altar with concealed clerestory over curving apse; entry in semi-detached tower. Beset with problems no doubt, this pioneering church (out of Ronchamp by Coventry Cathedral), obviously required national, not local interest and finance to save it. Bland replacement.

82 **Seaforth**, 1908, Linlithgow Road/Dean Road, Matthew Steele
Tremendously characterful and cleverly articulated flatted group, for R Simpson, spanning the corner has Steele pulling out all the stops. In murky Dorset pea rendering with chunkily random rubble quoins and insertions, it is the ingenuity and quality of the details, the access stairs punching through to the bracketed balconies and the loggias that give this block its originality and appeal.

Newtown, 1935, Matthew Steele & John Taylor
Built to re-house miners, estate of very basic harled, semidetached, two-storey, hipped roof blocks. Two stone blocks at entrance of estate with angled and parapeted projecting bay. Not much perhaps but Steele always looked to elevate the mundane.

Mount Stuart, 1 Grahamsdyke Avenue
Well-designed villa, amid luxurious landscaping and profiting by the exhilarating view over the firth, with a Spanish flavour: white render over red brick base, porch and terracing all under oversailing hipped tiled roofs.

From top *Recreation Centre; Bo'ness Academy; The Quarry; 73 Grahamsdyke Road.*

Redlands, 7-13 Grahamsdyke Road, *c.*1920
Attractive, although English in character, conventional terrace of four in red brick and white render, showing good proportions with advanced and half-timbered gables to street, swept dormers between. **Nos 3 & 5**, single-storey, semidetached block ingeniously raised to two storeys with large red tile-hung gable dormers.

Viewforth, 1890s
Another good stretch of bay-windowed Victorian terracing, on a sloping stretch of the road, in sooty stonework. The most easterly block with flamboyant parapet details and bracketed eaves over little porches.

St Mary's RC School, Gauze Road, 1955, Alison & Hutchison & Partners
Attractive design in frame and panel construction over buff brick base. Decorated brick service tower, zig-zag balustrading to fire-escape stair, all very Festival of Britain with its spindly details and pastel colours, amid some good landscaping.

Recreation Centre, Gauze Road, 1972, Alison & Hutchison & Partners
On sloping site, and now looking rather worse for wear, elongated metal box containing excellent collection of sports facilities.

Bo'ness Academy, 2000, The Parr Partnership
Extensive T-plan educational facility, on greenfield site with wooded background, for 1000 pupils in the same materials and aesthetic as its sister schools in Falkirk, Larbert and Braes (see pp.30, 59 & 101).

The Quarry, 71 Grahamsdyke Road, 1925, Matthew Steele
His own residence much altered; today whimsical bungalow with red tile witch's hat dormers

Top *5-12 Hopetoun Terrace.* Above *33 Hopetoun Terrace.*

Below *12 Dugald Stewart Avenue.* Middle and bottom *Drum Housing Development.*

flanking entrance. **No 73**, additions, (?)Matthew Steele, altogether more plausible. Sandstone and roughcast villa with interesting first-floor conservatory and open circular tower.

5-12 Hopetoun Terrace, *c.*1900
Elegant, well-proportioned and detailed dormered terrace, giving a feeling of New Orleans with its porch roofs supported on decorative cast-iron columns, a sensible and not often-seen gesture to a famous local industry. **Nos 17-18**, 1902, another attractive line-up of Victorian terracing, this one with shallow rectangular bay windows. **No 33**, a maverick, single storey in stone with huge arched window in advanced bay.

Erngath
Elegant gabled villa with hoodmoulded windows and spacious bay window.

Hollywood House, Grahamsdyke Road
Brash, opulent, two storey Dallas-style in chunky bull-nosed stonework with red-tiled roof over massive eaves; entrance porch and garage block adjoin.

12 Dugald Stewart Avenue, 1990s
Desirable residence – white walls, red-tiled split roofs and flower-bedecked balcony overlooking the waters of the Forth. A touch of the Mediterranean.

83 **Drum Housing Development**, 2001–2,
Wren Rutherford: Austin Smith-Lord
Ambitious layout of 244 houses, being first phase of Drum Masterplan by Anderson Jeffrey Associates, focusing on existing Drum Farm at high point of sloping site. Pedestrian pathways radiate out from central landscaped space to become vehicle/pedestrian mix roads serving the houses. One- or two-storey houses are combined with two- and three-storey flatted blocks. Mackintosh-inspired detailing, including projecting rafters, corner and gable windows, as used successfully by the architects at Irvine New Town, add interest and variety.

BORROWSTOUN

Old Borrowstoun, from which Bo'ness took its name, is now no more, engulfed by the modern housing developments north and south of Borrowstoun Road.

Borrowstoun House, *c.*1820
Curious slice of a house; two storeys with central bay window, steeply pitched and slated roof and moulded skewputts to its gable tablings; single- and two-storey extensions to its gables. Extension to rear includes circular stone stair and plaque to HMC (Henry Moubray Cadell of Grange).

Bo'ness Fire Station, Crawford Lane, 1981,
Central Regional Council Architectural Services
Compact design in concrete blockwork with chevron-pattern timber-cladding to first-floor dormitory block and fascia of appliance room; soaring four-storey concrete hose tower to south.

Deanburn Primary School, 1973,
Lane Bremner & Garnett
Single-storey design comprises flat-roofed pavilions, on exposed hilltop site, with concrete panel plinths, buff brick and deep fascias under pitched clerestory lights.

Above-average **housing schemes** in Grahamsdyke, 1964 Alison & Hutchison & Partners, weatherboarded finish between spine walls; **Mingle**, 1967, Alison & Hutchison & Partners, with tiled monopitch roofs, and in **Borrowstoun**, 1970, James Gray for SSHA.

From top *Borrowstoun House; Bo'ness Fire Station; Deanburn Primary School; Housing, Grahamsdyke Road.*

Carriden House.

CARRIDEN

Carriden House, 1602 onwards
In extensive wooded policies overlooking The Firth of Forth, horizontally extended four-storey tower house built over vaulted basement. In squared rubble with ashlar dressings, its most distinctive features are the four corbelled angle turrets containing cloverleaf gunloops and conical fish-scale slated roofs. Entered through spacious battlemented porch 1863, in the angle under elaborate plaque depicting the Hope coat of arms. The west wing, two storeys high, six bays long with projecting coping raised to form gablets over first-floor windows. Corbelled oriel windows overlook lush gardens to the east.

Within, exceptionally fine and deeply modelled late 17th-century plasterwork. Built for Sir John Hamilton, 1st Lord Bargany, who acquired the estate in 1607, and acquired by Rear Admiral Sir George Hope Johnstone in 1814.

Study ceiling, Carriden House.

Stables to west, 1818, stone courtyard block with arched carriage openings in symmetrical elevation with central tower. Single-storey ranges, mill with some machinery and mill wheel with undercut lade. **Walled garden**, 18th century, extensive enclosure with wall in mix of rubble and brick with arched openings. **Inner lodge**, 1818, restored, hexagonal plan, Tudorish hoodmoulded windows and grouped octagonal chimneystacks. **Outer lodge**, 1844, single-storey *cottage-ornée* with bay window and half-piended roof to west.

Romans at Carriden
There is ample evidence of, and literature on, the Roman presence in Bo'ness and its neighbours. Forts were built at two-mile intervals along the Antonine Wall from Carriden, sites at Inveravon, Mumrills, Falkirk and Rough Castle being now well-researched and investigated.

Carriden Roman altar.

Carriden Roman Fort (Castellum Velunia), 2nd century AD
Discovered during aerial survey by Dr St Joseph in 1945. East of the house and within its grounds, some 100ft above sea level, it measures 400sq.ft. Roman altar found nearby establishes the presence of a *vicus* or village community at Carriden.

Manse
With panoramic views over the Forth, large bay-windowed villa with arched entrance porch.

Carriden Parish Church, 1908–9, P MacGregor Chalmers
At the foot of Carriden Brae and with the trees of the old estate as backdrop, enormously dignified Romanesque building by one of the masters of that style. Aisled nave, chancel and apse entered through recessed arched doorway under four-stage tower with pyramidal stone spire. Under the barrel-vaulted roof, a model of the ship *Ranger*, once belonging to the Carriden Sea Box Society. Note many consecration crosses in the stonework, and within, pulpit, lectern, precentor's box and communion table, all executed in Romanesque as is

circular arcaded font; stained glass in apse, 1912. The Pieter Oostens **bell**, made in Holland in 1674, hung in the 1766 church and possibly in the original parish church at Carriden House.

Carriden Old Church, 1766

Picturesque ruin of galleried T-plan kirk in simple gothic. Tower and lucarned spire, *c*.1850, the north wall with aedicule protecting the Ionic **monument** to Sir William Maxwell of Carriden, 1771, laurel frieze. **Session house** to west.

Carriden Parish Church.

Carriden Old Churchyard

Includes many interesting mainly 19th-century tombstones, the chain-girt table tomb to Sir James Hope (d.1881) and a monument to the 'indefatigable' Dr John Roebuck, joint founder of the Carron Iron Company. Also, splendid cast-iron monument bears witness to the working practices of those times with the following words: *In loving memory of Maggie McIntosh who was accidentally killed in Love Stewart and Co No 9 Woodyard Bo'ness 10th July 1907 aged 14 years. A token of respect from her fellow workers.*

84 **MUIRHOUSES** ('The Murries' colloquially)
Hope Cottages, Acre Road, 1864
Very picturesque, well-thought through and exquisitely detailed group of eight *cottages-ornée* including girls' school, two-storey staff house and library, with Doric columns supporting its porch, built for Sir John Hope (Admiral Hope of Carriden) to house the workers on his estate. Simple vocabulary of stone walls, porches, half-piended and bracketed slate roofs and (very English) diagonally latticed windows make these very much more than the sum of their parts and an object lesson in the art of building (see colour p.88 and also the conservation village of Dunmore, p.69).

Left *Muirhouses Girls' School and Staff House.* Below *Hope Cottages.*

Grangewells.

Grangewells, Acre Road, 1911, Matthew Steele
A real gem, now beautifully looked after, built for
David Tweedie, Grange estate factor. White harled
with black trim and ingeniously asymmetrical, it
cleverly combines urban sophistication with the
vernacular. Steele's distinctive features are all here,
battered chimneystacks, decorative treatment at
copes, apices and eaves – not least the splendidly
audacious and unusual apsed bay window with
domed roof of the approach gable.

Bonhard, late 16th century (demolished 1950s)
Squat, L-plan laird's house, one mile south of
Bo'ness, occupied commanding site on high
ground. Built by Nicolas Cornwall, Provost of
Linlithgow (d.1607). House, mill and estate lands
were acquired by James, 4th Duke of Hamilton.

Airngarth Farm, 18th century
Red-painted ranges round courtyard; long low
west range with four-bay implement shed and free-
standing east range with full-length ventilator.

Old Bonhard Mill
Behind whitewashed cottage, picturesque pantiled
group with ruins of old mill building.

A
Adam, Robert, *114*
Adam, Stephen, 35
Adam, William, 11, *64*, 67
Airngarth Farm, 154
Airth, *3*, 63–6
    Castle, 64
Aitken, John, *41*
Alison & Hutchison &
    Ptnrs, 74, 136, 148, 149,
    151
Allan, Maxwell, 24
Allandale, 93–4
Almond (Haining)
    Castle, 103
Anderson, Sir Robert
    Rowand, 11, 29
Anderson Jeffrey
    Associates, 150
Antonine Wall, 7, 32,
    34–5, 47, 79, *86*, 89,
    90, 129, 147
Ardin & Brookes, 19
Arthur's O'on, 60
Austin Hall
    Constructions Ltd, 48
Avon Aqueduct, 107
Avonbridge, *87*, 108
Avondale House, 125
Avonmuir House, 104

B
Baird, Hugh, 41, 106, 107
Baird, John Logie, *13*
Balquhatstone House,
    110–11
Banknock, 93
Baptie, Shaw & Morton,
    122
Barr, Robert, *39*
Baxter Clark & Paul, 50
Beechmount, 51
Bellsdyke Hospital, 55–6
Bercott, Baron, 26
Billings, R W, *64*
Birkhill Clay Mine, 129
Black, A & W, 13, 25, 29,
    35, 36, 41, 42, 52, 55,
    59, 97, 108, 118
Black, Alexander, 22
Black, William, 17, 20, 21,
    25, *36*
Black Mill Inn, 61
Blair Lodge Academy,
    100
Blakey, Leonard, 39
Blanc, Hippolyte J, 77, 146
Blyth, J, 139
Bo'ness, *3*, 126, 130–46
    Cadzow Crescent,
        140–1
    Carnegie Library,
        139–40
    Carrier's Quarters, 137
    Cinema, 143
    Corbiehall, 143-4
    Customs House, 137
    Dymock's Buildings,
        133
    East, 145
    Erngath Rd, 142
    Gilburn Cottage, 145

Glebe Park, 140
Grahamsdyke Ave,
    143
Grange Terrace, 142
Grangepans, 145–6
Harbour, 133
Heritage Area, 138
Hippodrome, 133–4
Hope Street, 133
Hospital, 148
Iron Company, 137–8
The Knowe, 142
Library, 133
Main St, 136–7
Market Sq, 134
North St, 131–2, 133,
    134, 136
Ochil Tower, 142
Philpingstone Rd, 146
Potteries, 130, *146*
Public School, 140
Scotland's Close, *4*,
    131, 132–3
Snab Brae, 145
South St, *5*, 134–6
Stewart Ave, *88*, 141
Tidings Hill, 141
'Tobacco' Warehouse,
    132
Town Centre, 131-37
Town Hall, former, *136*
Town Hall, Stewart
    Avenue, 139–40
Union St, 133, 137–8
Upper, *88*, 138–43
Waggon Rd, 131–2
West, 143
    see also Bridgeness
Bo'ness & Kinneil
    Railway, *138*
Bonnybridge, 79–90
    Broomhill Rd, 89, 91
    Hospital, 80
    Seabegs Rd, 89
    Smith & Wellstood
        Offices, *86*, 89
    Wellpark Terrace, 89
    Wheatlands, 80
Bonnyside House, 89
Borrowstoun, 151
Borthwick & Watson, 96
Boucher, James, 25
The Braes, 72
Braes Fort, 72
Bridgeness, 146–57
    Bo'ness Academy, 149
    Cuffabouts/
    Causewayfoot, 146
    Dean Rd, 148
    Distance Slab, 147
    Drum Housing, 150
    Gauze Rd, 149
    Grahamsdyke Ave, 149
    Grahamsdyke Rd, 149,
        150
    Hopetoun Terrace, 150
    Kinningars Park, 147
    New Grange House,
        147
    Newtown, 149
    Pottery, 146
    Tower, 146

Brightons, *4*, 99, 100–1
Broch, Torwood, 71
Brown & Carrick, 100
Brown, Thomas, 23
Brown & Wardrop, 23,
    31, 33
Browne, G Washington,
    23, 53, 117, 139
Bruce, James, 5, *49*, 62
Bruce's Castle, 67
Bryce, David, 105
Burke, William, *102*
Burn, William, 60, 96
Burnet, Sir J J, 40, 52, 58,
    75, 119, 120
Burns, Robert, *4*, *19*, 58
Butler, Vincent, 45, 102

C
Cadell, H M, 145, 146
Cadell, W A, Architects,
    18, 128, 134, 135, 136,
    145
Cadell, William Jr, 44, *60*
Cadell, William Sr, *60*, 61
California, 108
Callender, J G, 15, 17, 19,
    25
Callendar House, 31–2
Callendar Park, 32–4
Cambuskenneth Abbey,
    76
Campbell, A Buchanan,
    34
Campbell, A Lorne, 142
Candie House, 107
Carriden, 151–3
Carron Dams, 60
Carron Grange House,
    60–1
Carron House, 62
Carron Iron Company, 4,
    8, *19*, 29, *59*, *60*, 61, 107
Carron/Carronshore,
    59–62, *63*
Carrongrove House, 78,
    86
Carronvale House, 52
Carselands, 69–70, *85*
Castle Cary, 92–3
Castle Rankine, 79
Central Regional Council
    Architectural Services,
    28, 42, 46, 73, 74, 89,
    91, 95, 96, 103, 123, 137
Central Scotland Airport,
    124
Chalmers, P MacGregor,
    36, 45, 153
Charlotte Dundas, 114,
    118
Cheape, James, 96
Churches:
    Airth, 66
    Airth Old, 64–5
    Avonbridge, 108
    Blackbraes and
        Shieldhill, 108
    Bo'ness Old, 139
    Bonnybridge, 79
    Bothkennar, 124
    Brightons, 100

Cairneymount, 102
Carriden, 153
Charing Cross,
    Grangemouth, 118
Christ Church,
    Falkirk, 29
Craigmailen UF,
    Bo'ness, 140
Denny, 73
Dennyloanhead, 92
Dundas,
    Grangemouth, 119
Dunipace Free, 78
Dunipace Old, 76
Erskine, Falkirk, 35
Falkirk Baptist, 22
Falkirk Old and
    St Modan's, 11
Falkirk West Church,
    25
Grahamston United,
    27
Grange, 121
Grangemouth West,
    115
Haggs, 92
Holy Rood,
    Grangemouth, *88*,
    123
Irving, Falkirk, 46
Jesus Christ Latterday
    Saints, 48
Kerse, Grangemouth,
    121
Kinneil, 126
Larbert, 49, 52
Larbert East, 57
Laurieston, 97
Limerigg, 111
Muiravonside, 103
Our Lady of Lourdes,
    Stenhousemuir, 57
Polmont Old, *3*, 94–5
Redding &
    Westquarter, 99
Reddingmuirhead
    Methodist, 101
Sacred Heart,
    Grangemouth, 120–1
St Alexander, Denny,
    73
St Andrew, Bo'ness,
    142
St Andrew, Dunmore
    Chapel, 68
St Andrew, Falkirk, 21
St Anthony's Polmont,
    Rumford 102
St Anthony's RC,
    Rumford, 102
St Catherine, Bo'ness,
    140
St Francis Xavier,
    Falkirk, 24
St Helen,
    Bonnybridge, 91
St James, Falkirk, 29
St John's, Camelon, 45
St Joseph,
    Bonnybridge, 91
St Lawrence,
    Slamannan, *4*, 109

St Mary, Grangemouth, 121
St Mary of the Angels, Falkirk, 45, *84*
St Mary of the Assumption, Bridgeness, 148
St Mary's Chapel, Slamannan, 110
St Modan (former), Falkirk, 36
Stenhouse & Carron, 58–9
Struthers Memorial, Falkirk, 18
Tattie Kirk, 17
Zetland, Grangemouth, 121
Clark Tibble, 19
Clifford, H E, 60
Club's Tomb, Linkfield, 70
Cockburn Associates, 14, 20
Cocker, Philip & Ptnrs, 95, 122, 123
Colville, Andrew, 133
Common Services Agency, 45, 80
Compston, 105
Conlon, A R, 24
Copland & Blakey, 13
Copland, Thomas, 15, 35, 38, 42
Crawford, A Hunter, 141
Cullen, Alex, 22
Cunningham, John, 129
Currell, A J N, 26

D
Davidson, Barbara, Pottery, 56
Davie, Alan, 117
de Graeme, Sir John, *11, 101*
Defoe, Daniel, *131*
Dempster, Mrs, 24
Denny, 71–6
Broad St, 73
Duke St, 75
Glasgow Rd, 74
Herbertshire St, 74
Stirling St, 73
Town House, 74
Dennyloanhead, 91–2
Denovan House, 76
Dobbie Hall, 52–3
Dollar, Robert, 39
drove roads, *104*
Dryburgh, 72
Dundas, Sir Laurence, 112, 113, 114
Dundas family, 112, 113, 114, 117
Dunipace, 71–2, 76–8
Dunipace House, 77
Dunmore, 67–70, *85*
Dunmore Park, 67, *84*

E
East Boreland Farm, 72
Easter Manuel Farm,

104–5
Elliott, Archibald, 33
Ellrig House, 109
Elphinstone Tower, 68

F
Fairlie, Reginald, 37, 57
Falkirk, 7–48, *81*
Aitken's Brewery, 20
Arnotdale, 39
Arnothill, 37–9
Bainsford, 28
Baird St, 45
Bank St, 15
Bantaskine, 40, *82*
Barnton Lane, 18
Baxter's Wynd, 16
Bean Row, 18
Booth Place, 18
Bus Station & shops, 19
Callendar Business Park, 34
Callendar House, 31-2, *82*
Callendar Park, 32-4
Callendar Rd, 30, 82
Callendar Riggs, 19
Callendar Square, 19
Camelon, 43–5
Camelon Rd, 39, 46
Canal St, 46
Chapel Lane, 25
Christian Institute, 21
coat of arms, *20*
Cockburn St, *25*
College of Further and Higher Education, 22, 30
Cow Wynd, 16, 17, 18
Cross Well, 10
Dalderse Cottage, 28
Darroch House, 40
Dollar Pk, 39
Dundee Court, 18
Fleshmarket Close, 10
Gartcows St, 35
Garthill Gdns, 37
Glasgow Rd, 45–6
Graham's Rd, 26–7
Grahamston, 26–8, *84*
Grangemouth Rd, 29
Great Lodging, 16
Hallglen, 47–8
The Hatherley, 38
High St, 10–19
Hodge St, 35
Hope St, 23–4
Howgate Centre, 14, *81*
Kerse Lane, 22, 29
Kilns Rd, 39–40
King's Court, 17, *82*
Kirk Wynd, 14–15
Lint Riggs, 12–13
Lochgreen Rd, 41
Manse Place, 15
Municipal Buildings, 26
Newmarket St, 20–1, *81*
Old Post Office, 23
Parkfoot, 34
Parklands House, 34

Pleasance, *7*, 35
Police Station, 24, 25
Port Downie, 44, 47
Princes St, 22
Prospect Hill Tunnel, 41
Public Library, 24–5
Rankine's Folly, 15–16
Registrar's Office, 20
Robert's Wynd, 15
Roman Fort, 35
Rosebank, 45, *83*
Royal Infirmary, 38–9
Sheriff Court, 46
Slamannan Rd, 42
South Bantaskine House, 40
Standalane Farmhouse, 41
Steeple, 9–10
Summerford House, 42–3
Sword's Wynd, *14*
Thornhill Rd, 29
Timber Hall, *34*
Tolbooth Street, 10
Town Hall, 26
Town wall, 9
Union Inn, 47
Vicar St, 22-3
West Bridge St, 25
Wilson's Close, 16
Woodlands, 36
Woodlands Road, 42
Wooer St, 10
Falkirk Burgh Architects, 33, 34
Falkirk Council Architects, 30, 33
Falkirk District Architects, 25, 44, 48, 57, 77, 132, 133
Falkirk, First Battle (1298), 7, *26*, 30, *101*
Falkirk, Second Battle (1746), 41
Falkirk Wheel, 5, *6*, 44, 47, *83*
Fankerton, 78
Fergus, Revd Thomas, *75*
Firdale Cottage, 105
Forbes, William, 31, *33*, 76, 77
Forrest, Robert, 20, 39
Forth & Clyde Canal, 8, 44, *79*, 106, 112, 113–14
Foster, Sir Norman & Ptnrs, 56

G
Garbett, Samuel, *60*, 61
Gardner, Peter, *70*
Garson, George, 117
Gauld, A, 15
GCA Architects, 64
Gibson, William J, 38
Gillespie, Kidd & Coia, 45, 148
Gilmeadowland, 104
Glenbervie House, 63
Golliways, Ruth, 100
Goodsir, J P, 52, 121

Graham, James Gillespie, 11, 16, 104, 125
Grangemouth, 111–24
Abbotsgrange, 120
Abbotsgrange Middle School, 122
Allan Davie Mural, *87*, 117
Avecia, *87*, 115
Avon Dhu, 119, 120
Avon Hall, 119–20
Bo'ness Rd, 119
Caley Bingo, 116
Docks, 114
Earl's Rd, 115
Kerse House, 113
Kersie Bank Ave, 122
Municipal Chambers, 118
New Town, 117–21
Old Town, 112–16
Refinery, *87*, 115
Ronaldshay Crescent, 120–1
Shipyard, 114
Thistlebank, 116
Town Centre, 116–17
Town Hall, 118
Victoria Public Library, 118
Westerton Rd, 123
Grangemouth Burgh Council, 122
Grant, John A W, 98, 99
Gray, James, 151
Greenhill, 91
Greenmount, 108
Greyrigg Inn, 108
Grubb, Kenneth, Assoc, 47

H
Haggs, 92
The Haining, 104
Hall, 79
Hallhouse (Holehouse), 78–9
Hamilton, David, 9, *31*, 32, 49, 54, 64
Hamilton, John, 15
Hamilton, Thomas, 105, 107
Hamilton family, *126*, 127-8, 130
Hare, William, *102*
Harlow Grange, 100
Hasler Farthing, 19
Hayes, Joseph, 110
Heiton, Andrew, 78
Herbertshire Castle, 77
High Bonnybridge, 91
Hodge, Albert, 58
Horspool, George & Ptnrs, 89
Howkerse Farm, 124
Hurd Rolland Ptnrship, 34

I
Inveravon Tower, 125
Irving, Revd Lewis Hay, *37*, 108

J
Jaques, Richard, 45
Jestico & Whiles, 34
Jinkabout Bridge, 125
Johnstone, Thomas, of
  Hallhouse, *78*
Jollie, Alan, Associates, 15
Jones, James & Son, *51*

K
Kay, William, 32
Kennedy Ptnrshp, 110
Kennedy, GRM & Ptnrs,
  37
Keppie Architects, 122
Keppie Henderson &
  Ptnrs, 38
Kersebrock Farm, 63
Kersie Mains, 69–70
Kinnaird House, 62–3, *84*
Kinneil, 126–9
Kinneil House, *88*, 126–8

L
Lane Bremner & Garnett,
  151
Larbert, 49–51
Larbert House, 54
Lathallan, 107
Laurieston, 97–8
Letham, 67
Limerigg, 111
Linn Mill, 108
Livingston family, *16, 31,
  32, 77, 93*, 98, 103
Locke, Joseph, 50
Lorimer, Hew, 24
Lorimer, Sir Robert, *127*
Lutyens, Robert, 13

M
McAllister Armstrong, 57
McArthy & Wilson, 24
McCracken, F J, 26
McCulloch, Felix, 24
MacDonald, Alister, 116
Macdonald, Sir George,
  98
McFadzean, T B, *27*, 37
McFarlane, Walter & Co,
  140
MacGibbon, David, 21,
  131
McGowan company, 58
McKissack & Rowan, 140
McLachlan, J J & P, 53
MacLaren, J M, 117, 119
MacMillan, Andrew, *45*
McNair & Elder, 22
McNay, C W, *146*
Macpherson, Archibald,
  120, *121*
Maddiston, 102–3
Mair, Alex, 124
Malcolm, A N, 73
Manuel, 106
House, 105–6
Nunnery, 106
Mary Queen of Scots, 32
Maxtone Craig, 121
Meikle, William & Son,
  122, 139

Metzstein, Isi, *45*
Millar, Gordon, 71
Millar, H & R, 139
Miller, James, 53
Miller, John, 93, 138
Miller, T M, 37
Mitchell, A G Sydney,
  124
Mitchell, A McC, 75
Mossmans, 11
Muiravonside, 103–5
  Country Park, 105
Muirhouses, *88*, 153–4
Mumrills, 97–8
Murray, John, 4th Earl of
  Dunmore, 68, *69*
Myrehead Farm, 103

N
Nether Kinneil, 129
Neuck, 66–7
Newton, 125
Nicoll Russell Architects,
  47
Nobel, Alfred, *97*
North Larbert, 54–6, *84*

O
Old Bonhard Mill, 154
Oldrieve, W T, 23

P
Page, G Deas, 22, 29, 46,
  121
Page, James Deas, 21
Page & Park, 123
Parkhill House, 96
Parr Ptnrship, 30, 59, 101,
  149
Paterson, G, 105
Paterson, John, 140
Paterson, Oscar, 142
Peddie, J M Dick, 146
Peddie, J M Dick &
  Walker Todd, 140
Peddie, John Dick, 110
Peddie & Kinnear, 12, 23,
  27
Pennant, Thomas, 4, *47,
  133*
Pilkington, F T, 54, 55
The Pineapple,
  Dunmore, *5*, 68–9, *85*
Pirnie Lodge, 111
Polmont, 94–6
Polmont Bank Lodge, 96
Polmont House, 96
Polmont Park House, 95
Polmont Woods, 125
Pont, Timothy, *3, 8, 104*
Porteous, A, 142
Powfoulis Hotel, 66
Pugin & Pugin, 24

Q
Quarter House, 72

R
Rankine, R W, 46
Red Burn Viaduct, 93
Redding, 99
Reddingmuirhead, 101

Rhind, David, *16*, 45, 92
Riss, Egon, 129
RMJM, 46, 47
Robert the Bruce, King,
  4, *90, 126*, 127
Robertson, W W, 23
Roebuck, John, 60, 61,
  127, 128, 146, 153
Ronald, David, 12
Ross, Thomas, 21, *131*
Ross Smith & Jamieson,
  40
Rough Castle, 90
Rowan, W G, 118, 142
Royal Scottish National
  Hospital, 53, 54–5
Rumford, 102
Russell, John, 10
Ryedale, 52

S
Scott, J N, 142
Scott & McIntosh, 145
Scottish Prison Service
  College, 100
Scottish Special Housing
  Association, 48
Sea Box Society, *144*
Seabegs, 90
  Motte, 90
Shieldhill, 107–8
Shiells & Thomson, 139
Silver Link Roadhouse,
  66
Simpson, William, 137
Skaithmuir Tower, *62*
Skinflats, 124
Slamannan, 109–10
Smeaton, John, 4, 113
Smith, James, 126
South Broomage, 51–3
South Doll, 70
South Kersie, 70
Spence, Basil & Ptnrs, 115
Steele, Matthew, 131,
  133, 135, 136, 137, 139,
  141, 142, 143, 144, 145,
  147, 148, 149, 150, 154
Stein of Bonnybridge, *91*,
  93
Stenhouse, 60
Stenhousemuir, 56–9
Stentmasters, *10, 16*
Stevenson, W G, 20
Stewart, Dugald, *127*
Stirling, Thomas, 25
Stirling, William, 64, 76
Stirling, Willliam II, 24
Stirling, William III, 39,
  55
Stirling County Council
  Architects, 30, 31, 51,
  57, 73, 93
Stirling family, *105*
Stoneywood Park, 78
Strachan, Alexander, 35
Strachan, Douglas, 58
Strang, James, 21, 24, 27,
  57, 75, 102
Strang, James, & Wilson,
  74
Strathcarron Hospice, 78

T
Tait, John, 22, 94, 113, 115
Tarduf House, 105
Taylor, Henry, 10
Taylor, John, 133, 149
Temple Denny Rd, 72
Thomson, James, 62, 131,
  134, 135, 137, 139, 145,
  147
Tideman (artist), 32
Tiendsyard, 125
Tod, Stewart, 69
Torwood, 71
Torwood Castle, 70–1
Torwoodhall, 51
Trysts, 4, 8, 17, 56, *57*,
  101, *103*, 107

U
Union Canal, 41, 44, 48,
  106, 107, 114
Upper Kinneil, 129

V
Vellore, 104
Victoria, Queen, *32*

W
Wallace, William, 4
Wallacestone Monument,
  101
Wardrop, J M, 32, *33*
Wardrop & Reid, 31, 33
Watling Lodge, 47, *83*
Watson, T L, 51
Watt, A, 27, 79
Watt, James, *128*
West Denny, 78
West Larbert, 53–4
Westfield, 70
Westquarter, 98–9
Westquarter House, 98
Wheeler & Sproson, 45,
  57, 74, 117
Whiterigg Farm, *102*
Whitworth, Robert, 113
Wightman, G, 145
Wilkins, William, 68
Wilson, B, 91
Wilson, Henry, 121
Wilson, John, 40
Wilson & Tait, 118, 121,
  122
Wilson, William, 139
Wilson & Wilson, 39, 73,
  118, 122, 123
Wolffe, A C, 33
Woodcroft, 51–2
Wren Rutherford: Austin
  Smith-Lord, 150

Y
York Building Company,
  32, 103

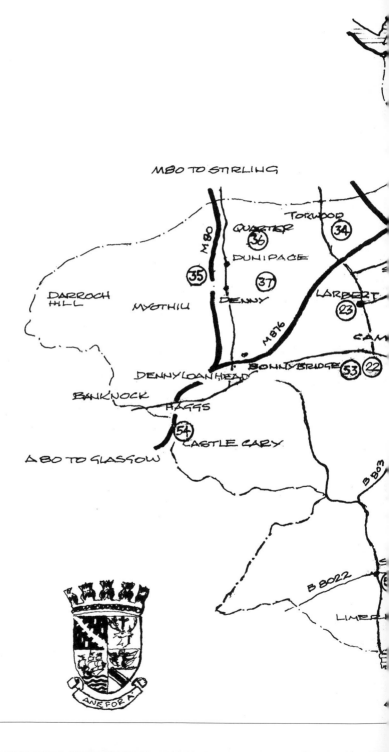

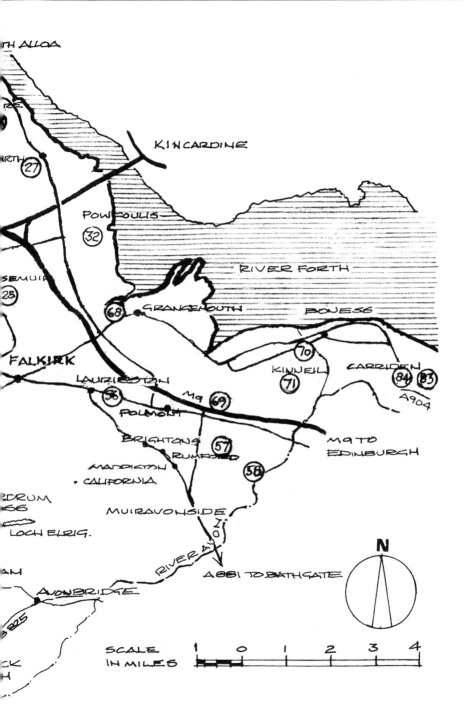

TH ALLOA

KINCARDINE

27

POWFOULIS
32

RIVER FORTH

SEMUIR
25

68 GRANGEMOUTH

BOUESS

FALKIRK

70

LAURIESTON

KINNEIL

CARRIDEN

58

M9

69

71

84 83

A904

POLMONT

BRIGHTONS

RUMFORD

M9 TO
EDINBURGH

MADDISTON

CALIFORNIA

57

58

DRUM
K56

MUIRAVONSIDE

LOCH ELRIG.

AVONBRIDGE

RIVER AVON

A881 TO BATHGATE

825

N

K
H

SCALE
IN MILES

0   1   2   3   4

ACKNOWLEDGEMENTS

This guide, as with all in the series, has been a collaborative venture and while, inevitably, the bulk of the work, together with its mistakes and inadequacies is mine, I have drawn remorselessly on the knowledge, help and enthusiasm of many colleagues and friends. The text was scrutinised by Charles McKean and David Walker, to ensure it attained the meticulously high standards required. Helen Leng and Susan Skinner of the Rutland Press also read and re-read the text, while labouring mightily with the nuts and bolts of publishing to budget and time. Stephen Downs of Falkirk Council has assisted enormously. My great thanks are also due to the editorial body of *Calatria*, journal of the Falkirk Local History Society, the articles in which were invaluable on the myriad aspects of the district's history and for their permission to quote from same: individual thanks to Beryl and Alan Naylor for help and hospitality and to Ian Scott, a fund of information and scrutineer of the text. Above all, I am hugely indebted to Geoff Bailey, Keeper of Local History at Callendar House Museum whose immense knowledge of the district and the help provided unstintedly and with great good humour over more years than I care to remember, encouraged me to persevere. Thanks also to Carol Sneddon at Callendar House Library, Janet Paxton at Grangemouth Museum, Stephen Astley of Sir John Soanes' Museum, Mary Tilmouth, David Witham, and Marischal Ellis of British Waterways. Thanks to Adrian Hallam and Rachel Black of the Almond Consultancy for wielding the mouse with such expertise and patience and to Stephen Gilmore, who chauffeured so willingly and expertly, *in extremis*. Lastly my thanks to Bill Cadell for his immense efforts and help over the years and for sharing his hoard of Matt Steele drawings with me; to Clare and Werner Gauster who made visits to the district especially memorable with their hospitality, and to my wife, for her eagle eye.

BIBLIOGRAPHY

Adams, I: *Salt Industry of the Forth Basin*, 1987; Bailey, G: *Falkirk or Paradise! The Battle of Falkirk Muir 1746*, 1996; Billings, R W: *The Baronial and Ecclesiastical Antiquaries of Scotland*, 1852; Bowman, I: *Symington and the Charlotte Dundas*; Bredin, M: *The Pale Abyssinian – A Life of James Bruce*, 2001; Buchanan, G: *History of Scotland*, 1582; Cadell, H M: *The Story of the Forth*, 1913; Cadell, H M: *The Rocks of West Lothian*, 1925; Campbell, R H: *Carron Company*, 1961; Dean, M & Miers, M: *Scotland's Endangered Houses*, 1990; Falkirk Local History Society, Scott, I (ed.): *Calatria* Nos 1-14; Falkirk Museums: *Bo'ness Potteries – An Illustrated History*, 1977; Fenton, A: *Country Life in Scotland*; Fenton, A & Walker, B: *The Rural Architecture of Scotland*, 1981; Fergus, J: *Forestars of the Tor Wood*; Fleming, J S: *Ancient Castles & Mansions of Stirling Nobility*; Gibson, J G: *Lands & Lairds of Larbert and Dunipace*, 1908; Gillespie, R: *Round About Falkirk*, 1879; Groome, F: *Ordnance Gazetteer of Scotland*, 1900; Haldane, A R B: *The Drove Roads of Scotland*, 1997; Hamilton of Gilbertfield, W: *Blind Harry's Wallace, 1460*, 1998; Hume, J: *Industrial Architecture of Scotland*; Hume, J: *The Forth & Clyde Canal*, 1979; Hume, J: *Scotland's Industrial Past*, 1990; Hutton, G: *The Royal Scottish National Hospital – 140 Years*, 2000; Kier, R: *History of Falkirk*, 1827; Lawson, L: *A History of Falkirk*, 1975; Lawson, L: *The Church at Falkirk*, 1974; Lindsay, J: *The Canals of Scotland*, 1968; Livingston, E: *The Livingstons of Callendar*, 1920; Love, J: *Local Antiquarian Notes and Queries*, 1908; MacGibbon, R & Ross, T: *The Castellated & Domestic Architecture of Scotland*, 1887; McGrail, S: *History of Airth*; McWilliam, C: *Buildings of Scotland, Lothian*, 1978; Marshall, R: *The Days of Duchess Anne*, 1973; Miller, T: *The Origins of the Falkirk Trysts*, 1936; Naismith, R J: *Buildings of the Scottish Countryside*, 1985; *New Statistical Account of Scotland*, 1845; Nimmo, W: *A General History of Stirlingshire*, 1880; Pennant, T: *A Tour of Scotland*, 1769; Porteous, R: *Grangemouth's Ancient Heritage*, 1968; Porteous, R: *Grangemouth's Modern History*, 1971; RCAHMS: *Stirlingshire* Vols 1 & 2, 1963; RCAHMS: *Exploring Scotland's Heritage – Clyde Estuary & Central Region*, 1985; Robertson, A S: *The Antonine Wall*, 1979; Salmon, T T: *Borrowstouness & District*, 1913; Scott, I: *Falkirk & District Royal Infirmary*, 1990; Scott, I: *The Life and Times of Falkirk*, 1994; Sibbald, Sir R: *History of Scotland*, 1710; Smith, C D N: *The Hatherly, Falkirk*, 1953; Smith, G I: *A & W Black, Architects, Falkirk*, 1991; Smout, T C: *A History of the Scottish People, 1560–1830*, 1969; *Third Statistical Account of Scotland*, 1966; Tranter, N: *The Heartland*; Waugh, J: *The Vale of Bonny in History & Legend*, 1981; Willsher, B: *Scottish Graveyards*, 1985; Willsher, B: *Scottish Epitaphs*, 1996.